Guide to Practical English for Culinary Arts

Edited by Kang, Kyung Jae

BAEKSAN Publishing Co.

This book is the seventeenth one which I have developed since I served as a professor. When this book was first considered, my objective was to have a publication that would offer various contents, data and information related to practical English for culinary arts which are needed to broaden our students' views on practical English for culinary arts.

This book has a total of 7 chapters which are Kitchen Tools and Equipment, Key Culinary Terms, Korean Recipes, Western Recipes, Chinese Recipes, Japanese Recipes, and Expressions Among Kitchen Staff Members.

In Chapter 1 Kitchen Tools and Equipment, there are two sections which are Kitchen Tools and Other Commercial Kitchen Equipment. Chapter 2 includes Key Culinary Terms. Chapter 3 introduces 13 Korean Recipes. Chapter 4 provides 18 Western Recipes. Chapter 5 covers 18 Chinese Recipes. Chapter 6 gives 14 Japanese Recipes. In Chapter 7 Expressions Among Kitchen Staff Members, there are three sections which cover Declarative Sentence, Interrogative Sentence, and Imperative Sentence.

I did major nothing relating to English Literature. I'm sure this book will act as an inspiration to always learn more, and encourage to gain confidence in studying English my student chefs who are eager to be successful in the culinary industry.

Nineteen years ago I was deeply impressed and shocked by the New Professional Chef 6th(ed.) which was given as a gift by one of my students,

Mr. Yang, Kyu Mo. In the book there is a didactic sentence that can't be forgotten even in my dream that is "A true chef is, among other things, a lifelong student, a teacher, a craftsman, a leader, and a manager." The book has influenced tremendously and will influence me continuously. As the development of food and cuisine has never been completely one-sided, so culinary education is not one-sided. Therefore student chefs have to influence the persons engaging in culinary education, and vice versa. I want to strongly emphasize that an interaction between student chefs and the persons engaging in culinary education is of great importance in culinary education.

In writing this book I have already promised to myself more improved and updated book will be published in the next edition listing a body of information pertaining to culinary industry.

I want to thank and acknowledge the following individuals for their help and assistance in the development of this book. The persons I have recognized here are some of those nice individuals from the culinary industry who were willing to share their experiences, knowledge, and expertise.

My special thanks to: Professor Kim, Yong Mun; Professor Yi, Chae Chol Professor Choi, Bong Sun; Ex-Professor Yi, Dong Hun; Chef patron Kwon, Oh Jun, Takumikon; Adjunct Professor Chong, Ji Yon, Hyejeon College; Mun, Sung Kwon, Chef/Owner, SamjungBonjum; Kim, Chun Hwi/Cha Un Sim, Consultant/CEO, Yoriae; Cho, Byung Sook, President, Hongsung Cooking School; Lee, Young Ju, President, Seoch'on Cooking School; Chong, Sang

Yun, President, Deomat FoodSystem; Kim, Nam Dong, Owner, Deomat Kukbab; Kim, Ki Yup, Chef/Owner, Sushi Good Day; Seo Dae Hui, President, GatesKorea; Chef patron, Lee, Chong Hak, Obiya Restaurant; Seo, Sang Yun, General Manager, Danyang Daemyung Leisure Industry Co., ltd.; Executive Chef, Choi, Byung Uk, CJ Foodvill; Chef patron, Ryu, Tae Hwan, Ryunique; Chef Yi, Sang In, Sheraton Seoul D Cube City Hotel; Chef patron Um, Sung Hui, Sushishouki; Chef patron Um, Min Ho, Umgane Komtang; StarChef, Chong, Ji Sun, Chinabokchun: Chef Min, Sang Hyun, Shuchiku of 63Bldg.

I offer my thanks and gratitude to the below individuals for their help and assistance in the development of this edition.

My special thanks to: Ex-President Yi, Chae Ho, Hyejeon College; Ex-Vice President Yang, Chae Gil, FoodCulture of SAMSUNG EVERLAND INC.; M.D. Shim, Hong-Bang, Director of Hospital, CHUNGJU MEDICAL CENTER; Dr. Yun, Sung Ro, Yun's Surgical Clinic; Dr. Kim, Man Gil, Gil's Dermatological Clinic; Principal Kim, Hang Sup, my close friend; Professor Cho, Nam Ji, Hyejeon College; Professor Yu, Kyong Min, Sunchon National University; Professor Han, Min Su, Hyejeon College; Professor Yi, Yong Hwan, Hyejeon College; Professor Song, Kyung Sook, WonKwang Health College; President Im, Kum Ran, Hwangje Food Academy; Chang, Hong Kyung, FoodCulture of SAMSUNG EVERLAND INC.; Professor Park, Ki Oh, Kyungju University; Professor Oh, Ch'ol Hwan, Kongju National University.

I would like to thank my family, my wife Ko, Yon Suk, my first son, Kang,

Byung Su(Bill), my only daughter, Kang, Dong Ok(Diana), and my second son, Kang, Duk(David) for their hard work, dedication, sacrifice, and assistance. Bill is working as a public health doctor of Korean Medicine at Inje in KANGWONDO. Diana is serving as an orthodontist at a couple of Dental Clinics in SEOUL and KYUNGGIDO. David is working as an intern at MOK-HURRY NECK*BACK HOSPITAL. Also I always thank for Bill, Diana, and David who are being grown up well and working very hard. Especially I want to appreciate my wife, Ko, Yon Suk, who has worked hard for our family, helping me with a precious and invaluable dedication to accomplish a better publication. As a result I complete the development of this book.

God bless you!

Kang, Kyung Jae
Professor, Division of Hotel Culinary Arts and FoodService
Hyejeon College

[Contents]

CHAPTER 1 **Kitchen Tools and Equipment** 11

1. Kitchen Tools _13
2. Other Commercial Kitchen Equipment _23

CHAPTER 2 **Key Culinary Terms** 27

CHAPTER 3 **Korean Recipes** 45

1. Gimbap or Kimbap _47
2. Jumeokbap _48
3. Gyeojachae _49
4. Seolleongtang _51
5. Oi Saengchae _52
6. Pajeon _53
7. Bulgogi _54
8. Galbi-Jjim _55
9. Jeyuk-bokkeum _57
10. Dubu kimchi _58
11. Yaksik or Yakbap or Yakban _60
12. Yakgwa _61
13. Sikhye _62

[Contents]

CHAPTER 4 **Western Recipes** 65

1. Greek-style Flank Steak with Tangy Yogurt Sauce _67
2. Mediterranean Kebabs _68
3. Japanese-style Beef and Noodle Soup _70
4. Beef Steak with Light Tomato Mushroom Sauce _71
5. Moroccan Chicken Stew with Couscous _73
6. Chicken and Mushroom Fricassee _74
7. Asian-style Chicken Wraps _76
8. Turkey Mole _77
9. Baja-style Salmon Tacos _79
10. Fish Veronique _80
11. Pork Mignons with French Applesauce _81
12. Pork Chops in Warm Cherry Sauce _82
13. Mushroom Penne _83
14. Linguini with Clam Sauce _85
15. Lemon and Garlic Pasta with Pan-seared Scallops _86
16. Classic Macaroni and Cheese _87
17. Corn and Black Bean Burritos _88
18. Broccoli with Asian Tofu _89

CHAPTER 5 **Chinese Recipes** 93

1. Chinese Chicken Salad _95
2. Crispy Phoenix-tailed Shrimp _96
3. Grilled Shrimp with Cilantro and Ginger Sauce _97
4. Beef with Oyster Sauce _98

5. Chinese Beef Stew _100
6. Spicy Stir–fried Hunan Beef _101
7. Braised Chicken and Mushroom _102
8. Cantonese Lemon Chicken _103
9. General Tang's Chicken _105
10. Fried Crab in Balck Bean Sauce _106
11. Almond Jelly with Melon _107
12. Apple–Blueberry Delight _108
13. Baked Fish Packages _109
14. Curried Fish _111
15. Steamed Salmon with Black Bean Sauce _112
16. Chinese Lamb Stew _113
17. Shrimp Chow Mein _114
18. Barbecued Pork _115

CHAPTER 6 Japanese Recipes 119

1. Tazukuri _121
2. Yaki Shiitake _122
3. Dashi Stock _123
4. Sashimi _126
5. Grilled Spanish Mackerel _128
6. Japanese Seafood Tempura _129
7. Japanese Simmered Pork Shoulder _131
8. Simmered Red Sea Bream _132
9. Chawan Mushi _133
10. Japanese Cucumber Salad _134
11. Ball–shaped Sushi _135

[Contents]

12. Anko Nabe _137
13. Nabeyaki Udon _138
14. Pickled Cabbage and Carrot _139

CHAPTER 7 **Expressions Among Kitchen Staff Members** 141

1. Declarative Sentence _143
2. Interrogative Sentence _147
3. Imperative Sentence _148

"Cooking is one of the great gifts you can give to those you love."

- Ina Garten (born February 2, 1948), an American author and host of the Food Network program Barefoot Contessa, and a former staff member of the White House Office of Management and Budget

1 CHAPTER

Kitchen Tools and Equipment

(Source: The kitchen of Pétrus, located in Knightsbridge, Central London, Retrieved 26 Jan 2019 from https://en.wikipedia.org/wiki/Restaurant#/media/File:Petrus_(London)_Kitchen.jpg)

CHAPTER 1

Kitchen Tools and Equipment

1 Kitchen Tools

Paring knife

- Small knife to peel fruit.
- Also good for slicing or chopping tiny foods.

Peeler or Vegetable Peeler

- Used to pare (remove skin from) fruits and vegetables.

Serving spoon

- Used to serve foods cooked in liquid.
- Also comes in slotted version.

Serrated Knife or Bread knife

- Saw-tooth blade.
- Used to cut breads and pastry without crushing them.

Pastry Blender

- Used to cut-in fats into dry ingredients.
- Also good for mashing foods like potatoes, bananas, and avocadoes.

Liquid Measuring Cups

- Liquid ingredients only!
- Available in various sizes, and also available in plastic.
- Place on a leveled surface and check at eye level for accurate measuring.
- The glass types are usually heat resistant and their markings don't rub off as easily as the plastic ones.

Dry Measuring Cups

- Used to measure dry ingredients.
- Usually come in 1/4c., 1/3c., 1/2c., and 1c.

Measuring Spoons

- A set of individual plastic or metal utensils : ¼ teaspoon, ½ teaspoon, 1 teaspoon and 1 tablespoon.
- Used to measure liquid or dry ingredients.

Graters or Box Grater or Tower Grater

- Used to shred or grate foods such as cheese or carrots.

Zester (grater)

- Shred ingredients such as parmesan, orange, and lemon into finely grated pieces effortlessly by using this zester grater.

Vegetable Brush

- Used to scrub vegetables and fruits, and to remove dirt and pesticides.

Pastry Brush or Basting Brush

- Used to brush butter, oil or glaze on food, and spread a glaze or egg wash on food, etc.
- Also used to apply marinade when grilling.

Muffin Pan or Muffin tins

- Come in a variety of sizes.
- Grease individual cups, or use with paper liners.
- Used to make muffins or cupcakes.

Can Opener

- Used to open lids on cans

Metal Spatula

- For evening off the tops of measuring cups.
- Also work well for spreading and frosting.

Turner or Offset Spatula

- An offset spatula, or turner, has a broad stainless steel blade that is bent to keep the users hands off the hot surfaces.
- To turn or flip food without piercing it.

Rubber Spatula or Rubber Scraper

- Used to scrape food from the inside of bowls and pans.

- Also used to fold in whipped cream or egg whites.

Mixing Bowls

- Containers to mix and blend ingredients.
- Come in several sizes.

Dish Drainer/Rack

- Drains Dishes after washing.
- Located under sink in each kitchen.

Rolling Pin

- For rolling out dough.
- Also good for pounding and smashing of foods.

Eggbeater or Rotary Beater

- Used to beat foods to incorporate air in such foods as eggs, egg whites, whip cream etc.

Electric Mixer or Hand-mixer

- Detachable beaters
- Used to mix foods that require time and endurance: whipping cream, whipping egg whites, mixing batter, etc.
- Heavy doughs will burn out motor.

Countertop Mixer

- 3 attachments: 1)Wire Beater - good for thin batters, 2)Dough Hook - for mixing & kneading bread doughs, 3)Paddle - good for cookies

& thick batter.

Whisk

- Used to blend ingredients smooth or to incorporate air into a mixture, in a process known as whisking or whipping.
- Do not use for thick batters or doughs.

Garlic Press

- Most presses require you to peel the garlic clove first.
- Also good for fresh ginger.

Cutting Board

- Protects counter when cutting with a knife.
- Can be wood, plastic and other various types of material.

Stock Pot

- Used to cook large quantities of liquid on the range, such as stocks, or soups.

Saucepan

- Straight sides.
- Deep.
- Primarily used for heating and cooking food in liquid.
- Come in many sizes in order to accommodate a variety of needs.

Dutch Oven

- This is a thick-walled cooking pot with a tight-fitting lid.

- Got its name from the early settlers who used it for baking cakes, casseroles, etc. over an open fire place.

Saute Pan or Frying Pan, or Skillet

- Used to sauté, pan fry and pan broil. The slope-sided pan allows the chef to flip items without using a spatula.

Wok

- Used for stir-frying.
- Once food has been cooked, it can be pushed to the side of the pan, leaving the hot center free for new ingredients to be cooked or heated.

Colander

- Used for rinsing and draining foods.

Strainer or Sieve

- Strainer can be used to drain pastas, vegetables, and stocks, or sift foods like powdered sugar, flour, chocolate etc.
- Strainer has wire mesh material.

Sifter

- Used to aerate dry ingredients for baking.
- Avoid getting the sifter wet.
- Tap out over garbage and wipe with a clean, damp cloth.

Cooling Rack

- Allows for better air circulation around cooling food.

Tongs

- Metal, wooden, or plastic pinching tools used to grab foods without using your hands or fingers.

Baster

- Used for basting (adding moisture and/or flavor to foods while cooking).
- Also used for removing fat drippings.

Kitchen Shears

- Snips foods such as vegetables, doughs and meats.
- Used only in the kitchen with foods, not for household use.

Juicers

- Allows you to get more juice out of citrus fruits than squeezing by hand.

Ladle

- Used for serving liquid foods and drinks.
- Also used for reaching to the bottom of deep pots and transferring liquids.

Masher

- Used to break up solid foods: boiled fruits or vegetables.

Food Processor

- Quick and convenient way to slice, shred, chop, mix, etc.

- Beware of very sharp blades!

Jelly-roll pan

- Basically, a cookie sheet with sides.
- Specifically made for baking cookies, cakes, and jelly rolls.
- Also good for baking foods that may emit a liquid, juice or fat.

Cookie Sheet

- No sides allows for even air-flow and cooking of foods.

Double Boiler or Bain-marie or water bath

- Cooks food over water (steam heat) rather than direct heat, which prevents scorching.
- Great for melting chocolate and marshmallow.
- Also used for egg and cream based sauces, puddings, etc.

Wooden spoons

- Used for stirring or turning foods.
- Wooden spoons do not conduct heat, and can be used in hot saucepans.

Pot Holders or Oven Mitts

- Used to protect hands when lifting or touching hot things.

Casserole Dish

- Used to bake casseroles.
- Used in oven and microwave only!

Egg Separator

- Used to separate the yolk from the egg white.

Meat Thermometer

- A short metal probe with a gauge, which is inserted into food and instantly indicates the food's internal temperature.
- This tool is used to determine a food's (roast, bread, etc.) doneness by registering its internal temperature.
- The most accurate way to determine if a food is cooked. Cooking foods to their proper temperature is essential to help prevent food borne illnesses.

Skimmer

- Has a flat, perforated surface for removing food from stocks and soups.
- Also used to skim impurities from the top of liquids.

Chef's knife or cook's knife

- Used for slicing, dicing, chopping, etc.
- Curved tip allows for rocking motion which helps with speed and accuracy.

9x13 Pan

- Rectangular baking pan.
- Used for cakes, brownies, etc.

Loaf Pan or Bread Pan

- Comes in a variety of sizes.

- Used for baking yeast breads, quick breads, and "meat " loaves.

Canisters

- Used to store dry ingredients.
- Comes in various sizes.

Meat Tenderizer or Meat Pounder

- Each side of a meat tenderizer has different-sized tooth-like points that are made of aluminum, steel or wood. These points tenderize meat by breaking up and bruising the fibers.

Pizza Cutter

- Used for cutting baked pizza into serving pieces.
- Also used to cut pies.

Meat Fork or Two tined Fork or Two tine Fork

- Used to serve meat.
- Also used to hold meats while slicing, and to turn solid pieces of meat while browning.

Apple Corer-slicer

- Push down over apple to core and slice at one time.

Pie Pan

- Used to bake pies.
- Sides are sloped in a pie pan, whereas the sides are straight in a cake pan.

Cake Pan

- Come in 8", 9", and 10" sizes.
- Has straight sides.
- Some have removable bottom.

Electric Mixer or Hand-mixer

- Detachable beaters.
- Used to mix foods that require time and endurance: whipping cream, whipping egg whites, mixing batter, etc.
- Heavy doughs will burn out motor.

Tube Pan

- Used for sponge and food cakes.
- It is a deep, ring-shaped pan with a tall tube in the center. The tube is hollow, with no bottom on it, to allow hot air to pass through it like a chimney.

Funnel

- Used for transferring ingredients to smaller containers.
- Also used to make funnel cakes!

2 Other Commercial Kitchen Equipment

Range

- Refers to the combination of stovetop and oven into one kitchen equipment.
- Provides heat for cooking food.

- Most powered by electricity or gas.

Refrigerator-Freezer

- Used to keep food fresh, prevent food spoilage, and inhibit the growth of bacteria.
- Every time it is opened cold air escapes; thus causing the motor to come on and lower the temperature again.
- Save energy by knowing what you are looking for before opening the door.
- Never cover shelves with something to keep them clean - air must circulate.
- Don't over load the refrigerator - air must circulate to prevent spoilage.

Microwave oven

- Cooks with tiny waves of energy called microwaves.
- The food cooks on the inside and outside at the same time.
- Most foods cook much faster in microwave.
- Less energy used.
- Not perfect for all cooking techniques (browning).

Food Mixer

- Used to blend and combine foods.
- Use attachments such as beaters, whips, slicers, graters, shredders, choppers and knives to make changes to the specific use of the machine.

Steam Jacketed Kettles

- Used to quickly heat, boil, or cook large quantities of foods such as meats, beans, soups, stews, vegetables, fruits, pasta, sauces, gravies.

Food Slicer

- Used to slice cheese and deli meats for preparations such as sandwiches.

Steamer

- Generally used for steaming food.

Turbo Broiler

- Used for broiling and roasting.

Steam-Jacketed Kettle

- Cooks large quantities of food using steam heat.

Gas burner

- Used for cooking the food by gas.
- Find in many size as you required.

Deep-Fat Fryer

- Also known as a frier, deep fat fryer or fryolator.
- Used for deep frying.

참고문헌

Retrieved Jan. 15, 2019 from https://www.sps186.org/downloads/basic/352989/kitchen_equipment.ppt

Retrieved Jan. 15, 2019 from https://www.gusd.net/cms/.../Kitchen%20Equipment%20MS.ppt

Retrieved Jan. 15, 2019 from https://www.ca-fcs.org/images/standards.../jbergdahl.Intro.Con.HTR.ppt

"Laughter is brightest, where food is best."

- Irish proverb

2
CHAPTER

Key Culinary Terms

(Source: Mise en place in a professional kitchen, Retrieved 20 Jan 2019 from https://en.wikipedia.org/wiki/Mise_en_place#/media/File:Mise_en_place_for_hot_station.jpg)

CHAPTER

2 Key Culinary Terms

Do you think you know every culinary term used in your kitchen? Here is the list of common culinary terms every student chef should know. Take a look at the list to get cooking!

Al dente:

cooked enough to be firm but not soft: ex) Cook pasta in boiling salted water according to package directions until al dente.

Bake:

to cook inside an oven, without using added liquid or fat: ex) Bake for 5-7 minutes in a preheated oven.

Barbecue:

to roast or broil on a rack or revolving spit over or before a source of heat (such as hot coals): ex) Barbecue fish approximately 10 minutes on each side.

Baste:

to moisten (foods, especially meat) at intervals with a liquid (such as melted butter, fat, or pan drippings) especially during the cooking process to prevent drying and add flavor: ex) Could you baste the turkey with pan drippings?

Batter:

a mixture of flour, eggs, and milk, used to make cakes, pancakes, etc, and to coat certain foods before frying: ex) Leftover batter can be saved for future use.

Beat:

to mix by stirring: ex) To make an omelette you first beat the eggs.

Blanch:

to put vegetables or similar foods into boiling water for a few minutes to make them white, remove the skins, get rid of strong flavors, or prepare them for freezing: ex) Blanch vegetables in hot water for 5 minutes.

Blend:

to mix or combine together: ex) Blend the ingredients until you have a smooth cream.

Boil:

to heat a liquid until bubbles break continually on the surface: ex) Turn on the gas to boil the rice.

Braise:

to cook meat or vegetables quickly in oil, then add a small amount of liquid and cook them slowly in a container with a lid on: ex) Braise 30-40 minutes or until the legs are tender.

Broil:

to cook something under a very hot surface in a cooker: ex) Broil lamb for 3 minutes per side.

Brown:

to make food brown by cooking it: ex) Brown the onions well but do not blacken.

Caramelize:

to cook (food), often with sugar, until a brown syrup is formed: ex) Continue cooking until the tomato paste starts to caramelize.

to heat sugar in order to turn it brown and give it a special taste: ex) Caramelize sugar in a small saucepan.

Chop:

to cut into small pieces: ex) Using a sharp knife, chop meat very finely.

Clarify:

to make clear by removing impurities or solid matter, as by heating gently or filtering: ex) To clarify stock, first strain.

Cream:

to make food into a smooth, thick liquid: ex) Cream the butter and sugar together.

Cube:

to cut (food) into small cubes: ex) Slice or cube zucchini if used.

Cure:

to treat food, tobacco, etc. with smoke, salt, etc. in order to preserve it: ex) Curing by salting, smoking, and drying are methods to prevent meat from spoiling.

Dash:

a small amount of something, especially liquid food, that is added to something else: ex) Add some butter and a dash of salt to taste.

Deglaze:

to remove the bits of sautéed or roasted meat and the juices from (a pan) by adding wine, stock, water, etc. and scraping: usually, the resulting liquid is used in or as a sauce: ex) Drain oil from pan, then deglaze pan with white wine.

Degrease:

to remove fat from the surface of stews, soups, or stock. Usually cooled in the refrigerator so that fat hardens and is easily removed.: ex) You may want to degrease at some point either before or after addition of spices.

Dice:

to cut food in small cubes of uniform size and shape: ex) Remove seeds and dice bell pepper.

Dissolve:

to mix a solid substance into a liquid so that it becomes included in it: ex) Add boiling water and stir to dissolve.

Dredge:

to sprinkle (food) with a powdered substance, typically flour or sugar: ex) Dredge lightly in flour, shaking off excess.

Dress:

to coat foods with a sauce, such as salad: ex) Prepare vinaigrette and use half of it to dress the leaves.

Drizzle:

to pour liquid slowly over something, especially in a thin line or in small drops: ex) Place the zucchini on the spinach and drizzle with the sauce.

Dust:

to cover lightly with a powdered substance: ex) Just before serving, dust with sugar.

Fillet:

to remove the bones from meat or fish. As a noun, a fillet (or filet) is the piece of flesh after it has been boned: ex) Season fillet with salt and pepper.

Flake:

to break or divide (food) into thin pieces: ex) Fish should flake easily when done.

Flambé:

to cover (food) with liquor and set it alight briefly: ex) Flambeed Pears are wholesome, saucy, sweet, and sophisticated.

Fold:

to blend (a light ingredient) into a heavier mixture with a series of gentle turns: folded the beaten egg whites into the batter: ex) Fold the corn mixture into the remaining egg whites.

Fricassee:

to prepare (poultry or meat) by cutting into pieces and stewing in gravy: ex) I'm about to start a large pot of turkey fricassee.

Fry:

to cook (food) in hot fat or oil: ex) Fry only a few at a time.

to cook in a fat is called pan-frying or sauteing; to cook in a one-to-two inch layer of hot fat is called shallow-fat frying; to cook in a deep layer of hot fat is called deep-fat frying.

Garnish:

to add something to (food) in order to improve its appearance or flavor: ex) Place on a platter and garnish with parsley.

Glaze:

to cover (foods) with a shiny coating by applying beaten egg, sugar, etc: ex) Glaze the pie with beaten egg.

Grate:

to rub food against a grater in order to cut it into a lot of small pieces: ex) Grate the cheese into a mixing bowl.

Gratin:

A dish with a light browned crust of breadcrumbs or melted cheese: ex) The gratin is done when it turns golden brown.

Grease:

to coat the interior of a pan or dish with shortening, oil, or butter to prevent food from sticking during cooking: ex) Lightly grease a pan with some of the flavored butter.

Grill:

to cook food over fire or hot coals, usually on a metal frame: ex) Grill them for about four or five minutes on each side.

Grind:

to process solids by hand or mechanically to reduce them to tiny particles: ex) Grind well and store in a small glass jar.

Julienne:

to cut vegetables, fruits, or cheeses into short, thin strips: ex) It can be minced or julienned for use in many different dishes and cold sauces.

Knead:

to work (moistened flour or clay) into dough or paste with the hands: ex) Lightly knead the mixture on a floured surface.

Lukewarm:

Neither cool nor warm; approximately body temperature: ex) Be sure to heat the milk until it is lukewarm.

Marinate:

to soak (meat, fish, or other food) in a marinade: ex) Let marinate for 2 days at room temperature.

Meunière:

(especially of fish) cooked or served in lightly browned butter with lemon juice and parsley: ex) We are going to do sole meunière with rice pilaf. Sole meunière is a very classic french dish.

Mince:

to cut or chop food into extremely small pieces: ex) Mince garlic and black beans together.

Mix:

to combine two or more substances so that they become a single substance: Add the eggs and mix thoroughly: ex) Mix well and pour over bread.

Pan-broil:

to cook in an uncovered frying pan over direct heat using little or no fat: ex) Pan broil the bacon slices until they are partially cooked and still limp.

Pan-fry:

to fry in a pan in a small amount of fat: pan-fried trout: ex) Or you may pan fry them on both sides in butter.

Parboil:

to partly cook (food) by boiling; to blanch: Parboil the vegetables in salted water for about 5 minutes: ex) Parboil carrots in boiling stock for about 3 minutes or until just beginning to soften.

Pare:

to remove the outermost skin of a fruit or vegetable: ex) Pare potatoes, let soak in a bowl of ice water for 2 or 3 hours, drain.

Peel:

to remove the peels from vegetables or fruits: ex) Partly peel cucumber, leaving strips of green.

Pickle:

to preserve (food or other perishable items) in vinegar, brine, or a similar solution: chunks of green tomatoes pickled in brine: ex) I intend to pickle them with Vinegar, onions and chili.

Pinch:

a small amount of something, such as a powder, especially the amount that a person can hold between their first finger and thumb: ex) Add a pinch of salt, pepper and nutmeg.

Pit:

to remove pits from fruits: ex) Peel, pit, and thinly slice avocado.

Plank:

to cook and serve on a board: planked salmon; ex) Pour the sauce from the pot over the plank.

Plump:

to soak dried fruits in liquid until they swell: ex) Cover with plastic wrap and leave overnight to plump.

Poach:

to cook something such as a fish, or an egg with its shell removed, by putting it in gently boiling water or other liquid: ex) We had poached eggs for breakfast.

Purée:

to make fruit or vegetables into a thick, smooth sauce by crushing them, usually in a machine: ex) Puree garlic and set aside.

Reduce:

to heat a liquid until it becomes thicker and less in quantity; to become thicker and less in quantity in this way: ex) Simmer until the liquid has reduced by about one third.

Refresh:

to run cold water over food that has been parboiled, or to place or keep (food) in cold water so as to stop the cooking process quickly: ex) Drain the spinach, refresh in cold water, and shake dry in a colander.

Render:

to make solid fat into liquid by melting it slowly: ex) This recipe calls for 2 pounds of rendered butter.

Roast:

to cook food in an oven or over a fire: ex) Many people like to roast chestnuts and eat them.

Sauté:

to cook food in a small amount of hot fat or oil over heat, usually until it is brown: Sauté the onions for five minutes. sautéed potatoes: ex) Sauté the chicken until golden brown.

Scald:

to heat a liquid until it almost boils: ex) Scald the milk and then add it to the egg and sugar mixture.

Scallop:

to bake a food, usually in a casserole, with sauce or milk. Crumbs often are sprinkled over: ex) I'd like scalloped potatoes with the lamb chops.

Score:

to cut ridges or lines into (meat, fish, etc.) with shallow slashes, usually in a diamond pattern, before cooking: ex) Scoring fish (when you make little cuts in the flesh) is one of the best ways to pack a ton of flavor into the meat.

Sear:

to fry a piece of meat quickly at a high temperature, in order to prevent liquid and flavour escaping from it: ex) Add the meats and sear on a medium high heat.

Shred:

to cut or tear in small, long, narrow pieces: ex) Wash and finely shred the white part of the leeks. When chicken is tender, use forks to shred.

Sift:

to put one or more dry ingredients through a sieve or sifter: ex) Sift flour 3 times and add to the mixture.

Simmer:

to stew gently below or just at the boiling point: Let the soup simmer for about 30 minutes: ex) Simmer on low heat for 1 hour.

Skim:

to remove a substance that is floating on the surface of a liquid: ex) Bring to a boil and, using a strainer, skim off the froth.

Slice:

to cut something into thin, flat pieces, thickness sometimes specified by the recipe: ex) Slice the mushrooms thinly and fry in butter.

Steam:

to cook food using steam: ex) Cover the pan and steam over low heat for 2 hours.

Steep:

to extract color, flavor, or other qualities from a substance by leaving it in water just below the boiling point: ex) Cover and allow to steep for 2 days at room temperature.

Sterilize:

to destroy micro organisms by boiling, dry heat, or steam: ex) Spoon into hot sterilized jars and seal quickly.

Stew:

to boil slowly or with simmering heat: ex) If desired, stew, covered, to tenderize the meat.

Stir:

to mix a liquid or other substance by moving an object such as a spoon in a circular pattern: ex) Stir the sauce gently until it begins to boil.

Toss:

to mix lightly until well coated with a dressing or until the elements are thoroughly combined: ex) Toss a salad.

Truss:

to tie up the wings and legs of (a chicken or other bird) before cooking: ex) Truss the chicken securely and sit it in the pot, breast side up.

Whip:

to beat (cream, eggs, or other food) into a froth: ex) In a mixing bowl, whip cream until soft peaks form.

Whisk:

to beat or stir (ingredients, especially cream or eggs) with a light, rapid movement with a fork or a whisk: ex) Whisk vigorously so the whites don't coagulate.

Zest:

to scrape off the outer colored part of the peel of (a piece of citrus fruit) for use as flavoring: ex) Here's the best way to zest a lemon like a chef.

참고 문헌

REFERENCE

Retrieved Jan. 7, 2019 from https://www.collinsdictionary.com/dictionary/

Retrieved Jan. 7, 2019 from https://www.merriam-webster.com/dictionary/

Retrieved Jan. 7, 2019 from https://www.macmillandictionary.com/dictionary

Retrieved Jan. 7, 2019 from https://en.oxforddictionaries.com/definition/

Retrieved Jan. 8, 2019 from https://dictionary.cambridge.org/dictionary/

Retrieved Jan. 8, 2019 from https://www.infoplease.com/dictionary/

Retrieved Jan. 7, 2019 from https://ueat.utoronto.ca/the-student-kitchen/kitchen-basics-techniques/glossary-common-culinary-terms/

Retrieved Jan. 7, 2019 from https://www.d.umn.edu/~alphanu/cookery/glossary_cooking.html

Retrieved Jan. 7, 2019 from https://www.youtube.com/watch?v=bsHeV1T4ERU

Retrieved Jan. 8, 2019 from https://www.youtube.com/watch?v=SRRtY928zWk

Retrieved Jan. 8, 2019 from https://www.youtube.com/watch?v=4YB-y4hakN8

"People who love to eat are always the best people."

- Julia Child (August 15, 1912 - August 13, 2004), an American chef, author and television personality

3 CHAPTER

Korean Recipes

(Source: Buddhist influenced Korean side dishes, Retrieved 15 Feb 2019 from https://commons.wikimedia.org/wiki/Category:Korean_temple_cuisine#/media/File:Korea-Seoul-Insadong-Sanchon-02.jpg)

CHAPTER 3

Korean Recipes

1 Gimbap or Kimbap (Dried seaweed rolls or Korean sushi roll or Korean seaweed rice rolls)

Ingredients

2 cups of cooked rice, still warm but not hot

5 sheets of dried seaweed

2 tsp of sesame oil

1/2 tsp of salt

2 medium carrot, julienned

2 cups of spinach, parboiled and chopped

5 yellow pickled radish, cut into strips (danmuji)

1 cucumber, sliced lengthwise

2 large eggs

How to prepare

① In a medium bowl, mix the freshly cooked rice with the sesame oil and salt. (Freshly cooked rice is best for gimbap.) Set aside.

② Stir-fry the cucumber, carrots, and spinach individually with a dash of salt over medium heat until cooked through, 2-3 minutes. Set aside.

③ In a small bowl, whisk the eggs until evenly yellow. Heat the pan over medium heat. Pour in the eggs and cook until almost set, 2-3 minutes. Flip the omelet in the pan and cook until completely set, about 1 minute longer. Remove from the pan and cut the cooked eggs into long strips.

④ Place a seaweed sheet on a bamboo mat. Spread the rice mixture evenly over the seaweed sheet, leaving a 1-inch border without rice.

⑤ Place the carrots, spinach, cucumber, radish and roll it up tightly using both hands, forming a tight cylinder .

⑥ Transfer the roll to a cutting board. Apply a little bit of sesame oil to a sharp knife. Using the sharp knife, slice the roll into bite-size pieces or 1/2-inch thickness. Repeat this process using the remaining ingredients.

2 Jumeokbap (Rice ball or Rice ball lunch box or Rice balls in seaweed flakes)

Ingredients

5 cups of cooked rice

1/8 cup of shiitake mushrooms, soaked and diced

1 large carrot, diced

1 large bunch of broccoli florets, diced other leftover vegetables like zucchini and perilla leaves (optional)

1 tbsp of soy sauce

salt and black pepper

1/2 to 1 tbsp of sugar (to taste)

1/2 tbsp of black sesame seeds

1/2 tbsp of sesame seeds

2 sheets of dried and roasted seaweed (crumbled)

2 tbsp of sesame oil

vegetable oil

How to prepare

① Stir-fry the diced vegetables with vegetable oil over medium heat. Add soy sauce, salt and black pepper and stir until vegetables are cooked.

② In a larger bowl, add rice, some salt, and sugar and mix well.

③ Add the stir-fried vegetables and sesame seeds to the rice mixture and mix together.

④ Add the crumbled seaweed with sesame oil and mix well. Season with some salt to taste. Shape into small rice balls.

⑤ Sprinkle some black sesame seeds over the rice balls.

3 Gyeojachae (Assorted cold plate with mustard sauce or Assorted meats and vegetables with mustard sauce or Mustard salad)

Ingredients

1 cooked chicken breast, shredded

3 cups of water

1/2 cucumber, deseeded and sliced into thin strips

1/3 carrot, peeled and sliced into thin strips

90g cabbage, sliced thinly

1/4 medium pear, peeled and sliced into thin strips

a generous handful of bean sprouts

1/2 cup water

1/2 tsp sugar

3 chestnut

1 egg

1/2 pine nut

For the mustard sauce

1 tbsp mustard powder, pinch of salt, 3 tbsp rice vinegar, 1 tbsp sugar, 1 tablespoon sesame oil

How to prepare

① Remove tops of the pine nuts and wipe the nuts.

② Pan-fry eggs for yellow and white garnish and cut it into the same size as carrot.

③ Take all the mustard sauce ingredients and stir the ingredients in a small bowl to combine. Let it sit for about 10 minutes.

④ Place the shredded chicken breast, vegetables and egg garnish on a platter roundly. Drizzle the mustard sauce over top. Top with pine nuts and serve. When it's time to eat it, mix all the salad ingredients together and dig in!

Tips

- Beef brisket and seafood such as shrimp and abalone may be added to this dish.
- Dip the vegetables in iced water for a crisp texture.

4 Seolleongtang (Beef bone soup or Ox bone soup or Slow cooked beef soup or Rice beef noodle soup)

Ingredients

1 kg beef leg bones or tail bones

800g shank or flank of beef

100g Chinese noodles

1 large scallion, cut into rings

6 cloves garlic, minced

Salt and ground black pepper

How to prepare

① Rinse the bones in a large bowl to remove any bone chips. Soak the bones and the beef in cold water for 30 minutes to remove any blood. Drain and put the bones and beef in a large pot, and fill with 2 liters of water with the ginger.

② Bring the pot to a boil for about 20-30 minutes, lower the heat, and simmer it for 3 hours, covered. Skim off any foam while simmering.

③ After 3 hours, remove the beef, but leave the bones in the pot and discard the ginger. Seal the beef in a container and refrigerate. Fill the pot back up with the remaining 2 liters of water and bring it to a boil over medium-high heat for another 3 hours, covered.

④ Turn off the heat, discard the bones, and cool the bone soup. Keep it in the fridge for several hours or overnight until all the fat floats to the top and gets solid. Take the bone soup out of the refrigerator. Remove the solid fat from the top with a spoon or strainer.

⑤ Boil the noodles until al dente. rinse with cold water, drain, and set aside. Thinly slice the beef, add the beef to the soup and bring the soup back to a boil. Once heated through, divide the noodles into serving bowls and ladle in the hot seolleongtang. Add some salt, garlic and black pepper to the bowls. Top with ringed scallions, and serve with warm rice on the side to make a complete meal.

5 Oi Saengchae (Korean cucumber salad)

Ingredients

1 package seedless cucumbers, sliced into paper thin discs
2 T sea salt
1 T Korean red pepper powder or flakes
2 T rice vinegar
1 T rice wine
2 T sugar
3 clove garlic, crushed
2 scallions finely minced
2 T sesame oil
1 T toasted sesame seeds

How to prepare

① Place the cucumbers in a large bowl and sprinkle evenly with the sea salt and mix well. Let sit for 10-15 minutes until the cucumbers have softened and released some liquid.

② Rinse off salt from the cucumbers in cold water, and gently squeeze out as much liquid as possible.

③ Place the remaining ingredients into a large bowl and mix well. Add the cucumbers and toss well. Taste and add more salt if necessary. Cover and refrigerate for at least two hours before serving.

6 Pajeon (Scallion pancake or Green onion pancake)

Ingredients

1 bunch scallions, halved lengthwise then sliced into 2 inch pieces

2 cups all purpose flour

2 carrot

1/2 teaspoon sugar

5 cups cold water

2 egg, lightly beaten

2 large garlic clove, peeled and grated

2 t salt

3 tablespoons vegetable oil, divided

For the dipping sauce

3/4 cup low sodium soy sauce

5 cloves garlic, peeled and grated

4 tablespoons honey

4 tablespoons rice vinegar

4 tablespoons water

2 tablespoon toasted sesame oil

1 teaspoon red pepper flakes (optional)

How to prepare

① Take all the dipping sauce ingredients and combine the ingredients in a small bowl and whisk together to let them mingle.

② In a large bowl, mix everything together but the scallions, and let sit for about 10 minutes. If the batter seems too thick, add a little more water (about 1 teaspoon at a time) until the batter is thin but not watery. Then add your scallions and give it one last stir.

③ Heat a frying pan over medium heat with a very thin layer of oil. Pour about half of your batter into the pan, spread the batter forming a thin pancake.

④ Cook for 3-4 minutes until the bottom is golden brown. Flip over and cook it another 3-4 minutes on the other side, add more oil, if necessary, until the pancake is crisp and golden brown.

⑤ Repeat with remaining batter. Place on a paper towel to absorb any excess oil, then slice them with a knife or pizza cutter into any shape you'd like. Then serve hot with dipping sauce. This dish serves as an appetizer or side dish.

7 Bulgogi (Barbecued beef or Korean BBQ or Beef BBQ or Grilled marinated beef or Sliced and seasoned barbecued beef)

Ingredients

2 lb thin slices of sirloin or other prime cuts of beef

steamed rice, optional

1 red chiles, thinly sliced

pinch of sesame seeds

For marinade ingredients

1/2 cup soy sauce

1/2 cup rice wine (such as cooking wine)

1/2 tsp roasted sesame oil

1 tbsp minced red chiles

1/2 tsp fresh ground black pepper

3 green onions, thinly sliced

1/2 tbsp minced garlic

1/2 tbsp ginger, thinly sliced

How to prepare

① Mix all the marinade ingredients in a large roasting pan. Add the sliced beef and mix well, turning them several times in liquid. Cover the pan with foil or plastic wrap and let the meat sit for at least 2 hours at room temperature or overnight in the refrigerator, turning several times to coat the meat thoroughly.

② You can grill, pan-fry, or BBQ right after marinating. If you're using an oven, preheat it to 375 degrees F. Remove and reserve the meat and pour the marinade into a bowl. Return the meat to the pan, leaving some space between them. Cook until tender for 40 minutes to 1 hour, depending on thickness, brushing with the reserved marinade every 10 minutes.

③ When done, remove from the oven, sprinkle the meat with sesame seeds and thinly sliced chiles. Serve immediately with steamed rice.

8 Galbi-Jjim (Korean braised beef short ribs or Korean braised short ribs or Beef rib stew)

Ingredients

3 lbs beef short ribs, rinsed in cold water

1/2 cup low sodium soy sauce

1/4 cup sugar or agave

1 asian pear, peeled and grated

3 cloves of garlic, minced

1 oz freshly minced ginger

2 tablespoons cooking wine

1 tsp sesame oil

1 teaspoon freshly ground black pepper

4 small sized potatoes, peeled and cut into large chunks

2 carrots peeled and cut into large chunks

6 pieces of chestnuts and dried dates (jujube)

6 pieces of shiitake mushrooms, stemmed and sliced in half

2 green onions, thinly sliced, for garnish

2 tablespoons toasted sesame seeds, for garnish

How to prepare

① Rinse the short ribs and let them soak in cold water for an hour or two to draw out some blood.

② Place the short ribs in a large pot and pour water so that all the meat is immersed. Bring the ribs to a boil on high heat for a half hour. Then, rinse any excess fat off short ribs in cold water and drain.

③ Put the clean ribs in the pot along with soy sauce, sugar, Asian pear, garlic, ginger, cooking wine, sesame oil, black pepper, and 2 cups water. Cover and bring to a boil over medium heat for another half an hour.

④ Add potatoes, mushrooms, chestnuts, jujube and carrots to the pot, cover and bring to a boil over low heat for another 30 minutes.

⑤ Serve in a big bowl with seamed rice and garnish with sesame seeds and freshly chopped green onions.

9 Jeyuk-bokkeum (Stir-fried pork or Korean spicy pork stir-fry)

Ingredients

400g pork belly or neck

2 carrot

3 large onion

1 courgette (zucchini)

1/4 small head of cabbage

4 tablespoons of soy sauce

3 tablespoon of gochujang

3 teaspoons of sugar

some cooking oil

lettuce or perilla leaves, for wrapping (optional)

For marinade ingredients

1/2 tsp of red pepper powder

2 tbsp gochujang (Korean chili paste)

2 tbsp of soy sauce

1 tablespoon of minced garlic

1 small onion

1 tbsp of minced ginger

1 tbsp of mirin

1 tbsp of brown or white sugar

a pinch of black pepper

How to prepare

① In a small bowl, mix all the ingredients for the marinade. If you want it more sweet you can add an extra half tbs of sugar.

② Cut the pork belly or neck thinly, the thinner the better. Slice the carrot and courgette and small onion, and then slice any vegetables you wish to add.

③ Put all of this in a large bowl, add soy sauce and the gochujang followed by the sugar (you can use honey if you wish). Mix together and put in a bag or box and refrigerate for at least 2 hours or overnight to marinate.

④ Let the marinated pork sit at room temperature for 30 minutes before cooking. Fry in a hot pan until well cooked, during cooking taste the pork and add more sugar to sweeten or add more gochujang to make it spicier at your choice.

⑤ Once fully cooked place on a large plate and sprinkle the pork with toasted sesame seeds. Serve with steamed rice and it is recommended to lettuce or perilla leaves for wrapping, now you're ready to eat!

10 Dubu kimchi (Stir-fried tofu and kimchi)

Ingredients

1/2 pound of pork belly or pork shoulder

1/2 pound of kimchi

1/2 onion

3 cloves of garlic

2 tablespoons of sesame oil

2 teaspoons of toasted sesame seeds

1 red chili pepper (optional)

2 scallion

1 package of firm tofu

a pinch of salt

some cooking oil

For marinade ingredients

3 tablespoons of red pepper powder

3 tablespoons of soy sauce

2 tablespoons of minced garlic

2 tablespoons of mirin

1 tablespoon of brown or white sugar

1 teaspoon of grated fresh ginger or 1/2 teaspoon of dried ginger powder

a pinch of black pepper

How to prepare

① Mix all the ingredients for the marinade. Cut pork into bite sizes. Thinly slice garlic, onion and scallions. In a large bowl, combine the marinade with pork, onion, and the remaining ingredients except the scallions and mix well. Let it stand for at least 20 minutes.

② While the pork is marinating, in a medium size pot, bring about 4 cups of water to a boil. Reduce the heat to medium high, and add the tofu and boil for 10 minutes. Carefully transfer the tofu to a colander to drain. Cut the tofu in half and slice each half into 8 pieces. That makes total 16 pieces.

③ Cut kimchi into bite sizes. In a well heated pan, add some cooking oil. Add the marinated pork and cook it on medium high heat until about 70% of the pork is cooked. Add the kimchi and sugar and stir them well until the kimchi is fully cooked.

④ When the kimchi is soft, add the sesame oil, sesame seeds, and the scallions and stir quickly. Remove from the heat.

⑤ Place the stir-fried pork and kimchi in the center of a large plate and circle the tofu slices around in a circle. Sprinkle toasted sesame seeds for garnish and serve. Or, you can serve the stir-fried kimchi and tofu side by side. Enjoy while still warm.

11 Yaksik or Yakbap or Yakban (Sweet rice cake or Sweet rice with nuts and jujubes or Medicinal rice)

Ingredients

5 cups of sweet rice

½ cup of dried jujubes

½ cup of chestnuts

½ cup of raisins (optional)

½ cup of brown sugar

3 tablespoons of honey

1 cup of water

3 teaspoons of soy sauce

3 tablespoons of sesame oil

1 tsp of ground cinnamon

¼ cup of pine nuts

How to prepare

① Soak the sweet rice in water overnight, then drain.

② Steam the rice for 20 minutes. Remove from the steamer and place the rice into a large bowl.

③ While the rice is steaming, score your chestnuts and boil them in water for 20-30 minutes, or until they are softened. Drain, peel, quarter, and set aside.

④ Drain the jujubes and quarter them, removing the pits inside.

⑤ In a small saucepan, bring the sugar, honey, and water to a boil. Turn off the flame and add in the cooked chestnuts, sliced jujubes, and raisins (if you are using them). Stir the mixture gently and let it cool. Check consistency and add more water as necessary.

⑥ Mix the soy sauce, sesame oil, and cinnamon, and add the mixture to the rice. Add the cooled sugar mixture and thoroughly mix everything together.

⑦ Pour all of the mixed rice back into the steamer, and steam for another 40 mins, or until the rice is fully cooked.

⑧ Pull out the rice from the steamer and shape into discs or press into a pan.

⑨ Scatter pine nuts over the rice. Serve when fully cooled.

⑩ These rice cakes can be served hot or cold.

⑪ If you wish, you can serve it alongside Korean Rice Punch.

12 Yakgwa (Deep fried honey cookies or Honey cookies)

Ingredients

1 cup of wheat flour

1 tbsp of baking powder

2 tablespoons of sesame oil

1 cup and 2 tbsp of honey, divided

2 tablespoons of rice wine

1/4 tsp of salt

1 tbsp of ginger, shredded

1/4 and 1/4 tsp of cinnamon, divided

4 cups of peanut oil

1/2 cup of water

pine nuts, for garnish (optional)

How to prepare

① Sift the wheat flour and baking powder into a mixing bowl.

② Combine 2 tablespoons of honey, the sesame oil, the wine, the salts, and one half of the cinnamon.

③ Pour that mixture over the flour mixture and knead lightly.

④ Roll the dough out. Use a round cookie-cutter and press it into the dough.

⑤ Heat the oil over low heat. Fried the cookies for 15 minutes, until the cookies rise to the surface. Flip the cookies over and fry them for five more minutes. Removed from oil and drain.

⑥ Mix remaining honey, cinnamon, and water to form a syrup, and let the cookies soak in the mixture for about 6 hours. Most Koreans like to add the powder of pine nuts to this Korean dessert.

13 Sikhye (Korean sweet rice drink or Korean rice dessert drink)

Ingredients

6-7 quarts cold water

1 lb barley malt (powder) (=barley germ (powder)

2 cups of sugar (adjust to taste)

2 cups of uncooked white rice

pine nuts, to garnish

1 ounce fresh ginger, peeled and sliced

How to prepare

① In a large bowl, combine malt powder and water. Stir well, then let stand undisturbed until all the powder settles to the bottom, about 2 hours.

② Meanwhile, cook rice according to usual method (in a pot or a rice cooker). When rice is fully cooked, rinse it in cold water to remove any surface starch.

③ Drain and reserve the clear liquid from step 1; discard the dregs.

④ Combine the clear liquid with the cooked rice, 1 cup sugar and the sliced ginger. If you can't fit all the liquid in the pot, that's okay, just refrigerate the excess. If you have a rice cooker with a "warm" setting, use that, or a crockpot set to "warm", or a very low oven (125-150F). Keep on warm 4-5 hours, until a few grains of rice are floating on the surface.

⑤ Separate the rice from the liquid, reserving both. Rinse the rice in cold water, cover and refrigerate. Pour the liquid into a large pot, along with the ginger slices. If you have leftover liquid in the previous step, add it in as well.

⑥ Bring the liquid to a boil, adding another 1 cup of sugar. Skim off and discard any foam that forms. Boil until no more foam rises. Remove and discard the ginger. Cool the liquid to room temperature, then refrigerate.

⑦ To serve, place a spoonful of rice and a few pine nuts in a glass or a tea bowl. Add the cold sikhye and drink.

REFERENCE 참고문헌

Retrieved Jan. 11, 2019 from http://messywitchen.com/recipe/

Retrieved Jan. 11, 2019 from https://www.coffeecatskimchi.com/

Retrieved Jan. 11, 2019 from https://www.saveur.com/

Retrieved Jan. 11, 2019 from https://messywitchen.com/recipe/

Retrieved Jan. 12, 2019 from http://crazykoreancooking.com/recipe/

Retrieved Jan. 12, 2019 from https://www.sbs.com.au/food/recipes/

Retrieved Jan. 12, 2019 from https://www.thespruceeats.com/

Retrieved Jan. 12, 2019 from http://www.chefssociety.org/

Retrieved Jan. 12, 2019 from https://www.everybunnyeats.com/s

Retrieved Jan. 12, 2019 from https://www.allrecipes.com/recipe/

Retrieved Jan. 12, 2019 from https://kimchimari.com/

Retrieved Jan. 12, 2019 from https://mykoreankitchen.com/

Retrieved Jan. 12, 2019 from http://www.hansik.org/en/

Retrieved Jan. 12, 2019 from http://www.koreaherald.com/

Retrieved Jan. 12, 2019 from http://www.beyondkimchee.com/

Retrieved Jan. 12, 2019 from http://aeriskitchen.com/

Retrieved Jan. 12, 2019 from https://www.thekitchn.com/

Retrieved Jan. 12, 2019 from https://www.thespruceeats.com/

Retrieved Jan. 12, 2019 from https://www.koreanbapsang.com/

"Life is like a sandwich. You have to fill it with the best ingredients."

- Unknown

4
CHAPTER

Western Recipes

(Source: A nouvelle cuisine presentation, Retrieved 27 Jan 2019 from https://en.wikipedia.org/wiki/French_cuisine#/media/File:Jacques_Lameloise,_escab%C3%A8che_d%27%C3%A9crevisses_sur_gaspacho_d%27asperge_et_cresson.jpg)

CHAPTER 4

Western Recipes

1 Greek-style Flank Steak with Tangy Yogurt Sauce

Ingredients

1 beef flank steak (12oz)

For marinade:

1/4 cup lemon juice

1 tablespoon olive oil

2 teaspoon fresh oregano, rinsed, dried, and chopped (or 1/2 teaspoon dried)

1 tablespoon garlic, minced (about 2-3 cloves)

For yogurt sauce:

1 cup cucumber, peeled, seeded, and chopped

1 cup nonfat plain yogurt

2 tablespoons lemon juice

1 tablespoon fresh dill, rinsed, dried, and chopped (or 1 teaspoon dried)

1 tablespoon garlic, minced (about 2–3 cloves)

1/2 teaspoon salt

How to prepare

① For the marinade, combine lemon juice, olive oil, oregano, and garlic in a large bowl.

② Lay steak in a flat container with sides and pour marinade over the steak. Let the steak marinate for at least 20 minutes or up to 24 hours, turning several times.

③ For the yogurt sauce, combine all the ingredients. Set yogurt sauce aside for at least 15 minutes to blend flavors. (Sauce can be prepared up to 1 hour in advance and refrigerated.)

④ Preheat oven broiler on high temperature, with the rack 3 inches from heat source. Broil steak for about 10 minutes on each side (to a minimum internal temperature of 145°F). Let cool for 5 minutes before carving.

⑤ Slice thinly across the grain into 12 slices (1 ounce each).* Serve three slices of the steak with 1/2 cup yogurt sauce on the side.

2 Mediterranean Kebabs

For marinade:

2 Tbsp olive oil

1 Tbsp garlic, minced (about 2–3 cloves)

2 Tbsp lemon juice

1 Tbsp fresh parsley, rinsed, dried, and chopped (or 1 tsp dried)

½ tsp salt

For kabobs:

6 oz top sirloin or other beef steak cubes (12 cubes)

6 oz boneless, skinless chicken breast, cut into ¾-inch cubes (12 cubes)

1 large white onion, cut into ¾-inch squares (12 pieces)

12 cherry tomatoes, rinsed

1 (4 oz) red bell pepper, rinsed and cut into ¾-inch squares (12 squares)

12 wooden or metal skewers, each 6 inches long (if wood, soak them in warm water for 5-10 minutes to prevent burning)

How to prepare

① Preheat grill pan or oven broiler (with the rack 3 inches from heat source) on high temperature.

② Combine ingredients for marinade, and divide between two bowls (one bowl to marinate the raw meat and one bowl for cooking and serving).

③ Mix the beef, chicken, onion, tomatoes, and red pepper cubes in one bowl of the marinade and let sit. After 5 minutes, discard remaining marinade.

④ Place one piece of beef, chicken, tomato, onion, and red pepper on each of the 12 skewers.

⑤ Grill or broil on each of the four sides for 2-3 minutes or until completely cooked (to a minimum internal temperature of 145 °F for beef and 165 °F for chicken). Spoon most of the second half of the marinade over the kebabs while cooking.

⑥ Serve three skewers per serving. Drizzle the remaining marinade on top of each kebab before serving (use only the marinade that did not touch the raw meat or chicken).

3 Japanese-style Beef and Noodle Soup

For broth:

4 oz shiitake mushroom stems, rinsed (remove caps and set aside) (or substitute dried shiitake mushrooms)

1 Tbsp garlic, minced (about 2-3 cloves)

1 Tbsp ginger, minced

1 stalk lemongrass, crushed (or the zest from 1 lemon: Use a peeler to grate a thin layer of skin off a lemon)

1 Tbsp ground coriander

4 C low-sodium beef broth

1 Tbsp lite soy sauce

For meat and vegetables:

1 bag (12 oz) frozen vegetable stir-fry

4 oz shiitake mushrooms caps, rinsed and quartered

8 oz udon or soba noodles (or substitute angel hair pasta), cooked

1 lb lean beef top sirloin, sliced very thin

4 oz firm silken tofu, diced

¼ C scallions (green onions), rinsed and sliced thin

How to prepare

① Thaw frozen vegetables in the microwave (or place entire bag in a bowl of hot water for about 10 minutes). Set aside until step 4.

② Combine all ingredients for broth, except soy sauce, in a medium-sized pot or saucepan. Bring to a boil over high heat, then lower heat and simmer for 15 minutes.

③ Strain the broth through a fine wire colander, and discard the solid parts. Season to taste with soy sauce.

④ To finish the soup, bring the broth back to a boil. Add the thawed vegetable stir-fry mix and mushroom caps, and simmer for 1 minute. Add the noodles and continue to simmer for another minute. Add the beef and continue to simmer for about 5 minutes or until the beef is slightly pink to brown (to a minimum internal temperature of 145 °F). Add tofu and scallions, and simmer 1–2 minutes until heated through.

⑤ Serve immediately in 1-cup portions.

Tip

There are several varieties of tofu, each with a different moisture level. Silken and soft tofu are the moistest and easily blended into shakes, dips, and dressings. Regular tofu is less moist, and it's best for scrambling or using like cheese in casseroles. Firm, extra-firm, and pressed tofus are the driest. They absorb other flavors easily and hold their shape in stir-fries and on the grill.

4 Beef Steak with Light Tomato Mushroom Sauce

Ingredients

1 Tbsp olive oil

4 beef top sirloin steaks, lean (3 oz each)

4 oz white mushrooms, rinsed and quartered (about 1 C)

1 large shallot, minced (about 2 Tbsp)

1 Tbsp garlic, minced (about 2 – 3 cloves)

1 C canned no-salt-added diced tomatoes

2 Tbsp no-salt-added tomato paste

2 Tbsp apple cider vinegar

2 C low-sodium beef broth

1 Tbsp cornstarch

1 Tbsp fresh parsley, rinsed, dried, and minced (or 1 tsp dried)

1 Tbsp fresh tarragon, rinsed, dried, and chopped (or 1 tsp dried)

½ tsp salt

¼ tsp ground black pepper

How to prepare

① Preheat oven to 350 °F. Heat olive oil in a large, heavy-bottom sauté pan.

② Gently blot steaks dry with paper towels and then carefully place them in the hot pan. Sauté both sides, about 2 – 3 minutes, until golden to dark brown.

③ Remove steaks from pan, and put them on a baking sheet to finish in the preheated oven for an additional 3 – 5 minutes or to your desired doneness (to a minimum internal temperature of 145 °F).

④ To make the sauce, pour off any excess grease from the pan. Add mushrooms and sauté until lightly brown, about 3-4 minutes. Lower the heat, and add shallot and garlic. Cook gently over low heat for about 2 minutes, until tender, but not brown. Add tomatoes, tomato paste, and apple cider vinegar, and cook an additional 3 minutes.

⑤ In a bowl, mix beef broth and cornstarch. Add broth mixture, parsley and tarragon to the sauté pan. Bring to a boil on medium-high heat while stirring constantly. Lower the heat and simmer for 2-3 minutes.

⑥ Season with salt and pepper. Serve one steak with ½ cup sauce.

5 Moroccan Chicken Stew With Couscous

Ingredients

1 Tbsp olive oil

1 lb skinless chicken legs, split (about 4 whole legs)

1 Tbsp Moroccan spice blend*

1 C carrots, rinsed, peeled, and diced

1 C onion, diced

¼ C lemon juice

2 C low-sodium chicken broth

½ C ripe black olives, sliced

¼ tsp salt

1 Tbsp chili sauce (optional)

For couscous:

1 C low-sodium chicken broth

1 C couscous (try whole-wheat couscous)

1 Tbsp fresh mint, rinsed, dried, and shredded thin (or 1 tsp dried)

How to prepare

① Heat olive oil in a large sauté pan. Add chicken legs, and brown on all sides, about 2–3 minutes per side. Remove chicken from pan and put on a plate with a cover to hold warm.

② Add spice blend to sauté pan and toast gently. Add carrots and onion to sauté pan, and cook for about 3–4 minutes or until the onions have turned clear, but not brown. Add lemon juice, chicken broth, and olives to sauté pan, and bring to a boil over high heat. Add chicken legs, and return to a boil. Cover and gently simmer for about 10–15 minutes (to a minimum internal temperature of 165 °F).

③ Meanwhile, prepare the couscous by bringing chicken broth to a boil in a saucepan. Add couscous and remove from the heat. Cover and let stand for 10 minutes.

④ Fluff couscous with a fork, and gently mix in the mint.

⑤ When chicken is cooked, add salt. Serve two chicken legs over ½ cup couscous topped with ½ cup sauce in a serving bowl. Add chili sauce to taste.

* You also can make your own Moroccan spice blend by mixing 1 teaspoon each of ground coriander, ground cumin, ground ginger, and ground cinnamon per 1 pound of meat or chicken. Make this mix in advance and store it in your pantry to use as needed.

6 Chicken and Mushroom Fricassee

Ingredients

1 Tbsp olive oil

1 carton (10 oz) white button mushrooms, rinsed and quartered

1 C leeks, split into quarters, then sliced into small squares and rinsed well

1 C potatoes, peeled and diced

1 C celery, rinsed and diced

1 C pearl onions, raw or frozen

3 C low-sodium chicken broth

1 lb skinless chicken legs or thighs (4 whole legs, split, or 8 thighs)

2 Tbsp each fresh herbs (such as parsley and chives), rinsed, dried, and

minced (or 2 tsp dried)

1 Tbsp lemon juice

1 Tbsp cornstarch

2 Tbsp fat-free sour cream

½ tsp salt

¼ tsp ground black pepper

How to prepare

① Preheat oven to 350 °F. Heat olive oil in a medium-sized heavy-bottom roasting or braising pan (a large sauté pan with a metal handle will work as well).

② Add mushrooms to pan, and cook until golden brown, about 3–5 minutes. Add leeks, potatoes, celery, and pearl onions, and continue to cook until the vegetables become soft, about 3–5 additional minutes.

③ Add chicken broth to the pan, and bring to a boil. Add chicken legs to the pan, cover, and place in the heated oven for about 20 minutes or until the chicken legs are tender when pierced with a fork (to a minimum internal temperature of 165 °F).

④ When chicken legs are tender, remove legs from the pan, return the pan to the stovetop, and bring the liquid to a boil. Add herbs and lemon juice.

⑤ In a bowl, mix the cornstarch with the sour cream, and add to the pan. Bring back to a boil and then remove from the heat.

⑥ Season with salt and pepper, and pour 1 cup of vegetables and sauce over chicken.

7 Asian-style Chicken Wraps

For sauce:

1 small Jalapeno chili pepper, rinsed and split lengthwise— remove seeds and white membrane, and mince (about 1 Tbsp); for less spice, use green bell pepper

1 Tbsp garlic, minced (about 2–3 cloves)

3 Tbsp brown sugar or honey

½ C water

½ Tbsp fish sauce

2 Tbsp lime juice (or about 4 limes)

For chicken:

1 Tbsp peanut oil or vegetable oil

1 Tbsp ginger, minced

1 Tbsp garlic, minced (about 2–3 cloves)

12 oz boneless, skinless chicken breast, cut into thin strips

1 Tbsp lite soy sauce

1 Tbsp sesame oil (optional)

1 Tbsp sesame seeds (optional)

For wrap:

1 (small) head red leaf lettuce, rinsed, dried, and separated into single leaves large enough to create wrap

8 fresh basil leaves, whole, rinsed and dried

2 C bok choy or Asian cabbage, rinsed and shredded

How to prepare

① To prepare the sauce, add all ingredients to a saucepan, and bring to a boil over high heat. Remove from heat, and let sit in hot saucepan for 3–5 minutes. Chill in refrigerator for about 15 minutes or until cold.

② Prepare the chicken by heating oil in a large wok or sauté pan. Add ginger and garlic, and stir fry briefly until cooked but not brown, about 30 seconds to 1 minute. Add chicken, and continue to stir fry for 5–8 minutes. Add soy sauce, sesame oil (optional), and sesame seeds (optional), and return to a boil. Remove from the heat, and cover with lid to hold warm in hot sauté pan.

③ Assemble each wrap: Place one large red lettuce leaf on a plate, then add ½ cup chicken stir-fry, 1 basil leaf, and ¼ cup shredded cabbage and fold together. Serve two wraps with ¼ cup sauce.

8 Turkey Mole

For sauce:

1 Tbsp chili powder

1 tsp ground black pepper

1/8 tsp ground cloves

1/8 tsp ground allspice

1 Tbsp sesame seeds (reserve 1 tsp for garnish) (optional)

2 Tbsp canola oil, divided into two 1-Tbsp portions

½ Tbsp garlic, minced (about 1 clove)

½ C onion, chopped

1 C canned no-salt-added diced tomatoes

1 tsp fresh oregano, rinsed, dried, and chopped (or ¼ tsp dried)

1 Tbsp cocoa powder

1 C low-sodium chicken broth

For turkey:

12 oz turkey fillets, boneless and skinless (about 4 pieces)

½ tsp salt

½ tsp ground black pepper

How to prepare

① Preheat grill pan or oven broiler (with the rack 3 inches from heat source) on high temperature.

② To prepare the sauce, add chili powder, pepper, cloves, allspice, and sesame seeds (optional) to a saucepan, and toast on medium heat for 2 minutes. Add 1 tablespoon canola oil. Sauté garlic on medium to medium-high heat for 30 seconds to 1 minute. Add onion, and sauté until cooked but not brown, about 2–3 minutes. Add tomatoes, oregano, cocoa powder, and chicken broth, and bring to a boil over high heat. Simmer for 8–10 minutes.

③ Remove from the heat, and let cool to room temperature. Puree the sauce in a blender until smooth. Return sauce to the pan, and reheat slowly (or keep sauce warm on stovetop).

④ To prepare the turkey, coat the fillets with 1 tablespoon canola oil and season with salt and pepper. Broil turkey in preheated oven or grill for 3–5 minutes on each side or until the turkey is fully cooked (to a minimum internal temperature of 165 °F).

⑤ Serve one piece of turkey with ½ cup of the warm mole sauce.

9 Baja-style Salmon Tacos

Ingredients

12 oz salmon fillet, cut into 4 portions (3 oz each)

4 (8-inch) whole-wheat tortillas

For taco filling:

1 C green cabbage (about ¼ head), rinsed and shredded

1 tsp lime juice

1 tsp honey

½ C red onion, thinly sliced (or substitute white onion)

1 medium Jalapeno chili pepper, rinsed and split lengthwise—remove seeds and white membrane, and mince (about 2 Tbsp); for less spice, use green bell pepper

1 tsp fresh cilantro, minced (or substitute ½ tsp ground coriander)

For marinade:

½ Tbsp corn oil or other vegetable oil

1 Tbsp lime juice

2 tsp chili powder

½ tsp ground cumin

½ tsp ground coriander

¼ tsp salt

How to prepare

① Preheat grill or oven broiler (with the rack 3 inches from heat source) on high temperature.

② Prepare taco filling by combining all ingredients. Let stand for 10–15 minutes to blend the flavors.

③ To prepare the marinade, combine the oil, lime juice, chili powder, cumin, coriander, and salt in a bowl.

④ Place salmon fillets in a flat dish with sides. Pour marinade evenly over fillets. Place salmon fillets on grill or broiler. Cook for 3–4 minutes on each side, until fish flakes easily with a fork in the thickest part (to a minimum internal temperature of 145 °F). Remove from the heat and set aside for 2–3 minutes. Cut into strips.

⑤ To make each taco, fill one tortilla with ¾ cup filling and one salmon fillet.

10 Fish Veronique

Ingredients

12 oz white fish (such as cod, sole, or turbot),
cut into 4 portions (3 oz each)
¼ tsp salt
1/8 tsp ground black pepper
¼ C dry white wine
¼ C chicken broth; skim fat from the top
1 Tbsp lemon juice
1 Tbsp soft tub margarine
2 Tbsp flour
¾ C low-fat (1 percent) or fat-free milk
½ C seedless grapes, rinsed
Cooking spray

How to prepare

① Preheat oven to 350 °F. Spray a 10- by 6-inch baking dish with cooking spray. Place fish in dish, and sprinkle with salt and pepper.

② Mix wine, chicken broth, and lemon juice in a small bowl, and pour over fish. Cover and bake at 350 °F for 15 minutes.

③ Meanwhile, melt margarine in a small saucepan. Remove from heat and blend in flour. Gradually add milk. Return to stovetop and cook over moderately low heat, stirring constantly, until thickened.

④ Remove fish from oven, and pour liquid from baking dish into "cream" sauce, stirring until blended. Pour sauce over fish and sprinkle with grapes.

⑤ Broil about 3 inches from heat for 5 minutes or until sauce starts to brown (and fish reaches a minimum internal temperature of 145 °F).

⑥ Serve one fillet with sauce.

11 Pork Mignons with French Applesauce

Ingredients

1 pair pork tenderloins (about 2 lb)

¼ tsp salt

1/8 tsp ground black pepper

2 medium apples, rinsed and cored, but not peeled (try Golden Delicious or Rome)

2 Tbsp dark seedless raisins

2 Tbsp walnuts, broken into coarse pieces

½ tsp cinnamon

Cooking spray

How to prepare

① Preheat oven broiler on high temperature, with the rack 3 inches from heat source. Cover broiler pan with aluminum foil for easy cleanup. Spray foil lightly with cooking spray. Set aside.

② Cut 8 slices (pork rounds), each 1½ inches thick, from the center of the pair of pork tenderloins. Refrigerate or freeze the ends for another use. Place pork rounds on the foil-covered broiler pan. Sprinkle with salt and pepper. Set aside a few minutes while broiler heats.

③ Meanwhile, heat ½ cup water to boiling in a medium nonstick pan. Slice cored apples from top to bottom in ¼-inch wide pieces. Add apples, raisins, walnuts, and cinnamon to boiling water. Reduce heat to medium. Cover. Simmer, stirring occasionally, until apples are soft and easily pierced with a fork. Set aside until pork is cooked.

④ Broil pork for 5–10 minutes per side (to a minimum internal temperature of 160 °F).

⑤ To serve, place two pork rounds on each dinner plate. Top with one-fourth of the applesauce.

12 Pork Chops in Warm Cherry Sauce

Ingredients

4 bone-in center-cut pork chops (about 5 oz each)

¼ tsp salt

1/8 tsp ground black pepper

2 tsp olive oil, divided into 1½ tsp and ½ tsp portions

1 C onion, diced

1 C dry red wine

1 tsp dried tarragon

1 C dried cherries, either sweet Bing or tart (or substitute another dried fruit such as raisins, figs, or prunes)

How to prepare

① Trim visible fat from pork chops. Sprinkle with salt and pepper.

② In a large nonstick pan, warm 1½ teaspoons of oil over high heat. When pan is hot, brown chops on both sides, about 2 minutes per side. Remove chops from pan. Set aside.

③ Over medium heat, add remaining ½ teaspoon of oil and diced onion. Cook and stir until onion softens, about 5 minutes.

④ Add red wine. Cook and stir 1 minute to loosen the flavorful brown bits and mix them into the sauce. Add tarragon and cherries. Cook and stir 1 minute to blend.

⑤ Return pork chops and any juices to pan. Cover. Simmer 9 minutes to thicken sauce and until pork chops are fully cooked (to a minimum internal temperature of 160 °F).

⑥ Serve immediately.

13 Mushroom Penne

Ingredients

8 oz whole-wheat penne pasta

2 Tbsp olive oil

8 oz white mushrooms, rinsed and sliced

½ C onion, thinly sliced

1 Tbsp garlic, minced or pressed (about 2-3 cloves)

6 Tbsp dry red wine

1 C low-sodium chicken broth

¼ tsp salt

¼ tsp ground black pepper

1 tsp dried thyme

4 Tbsp shredded parmesan cheese

How to prepare

① In a 4-quart saucepan, bring 3 quarts of water to a boil over high heat.

② Add pasta, and cook according to package directions for the shortest recommended time, about 8 minutes.

③ While water heats and pasta cooks, warm olive oil in a large nonstick pan over medium heat.

④ Chop the mushrooms into bite-sized pieces. Cook the mushrooms in the oil for 5 minutes.

⑤ Meanwhile, slice onion and mince garlic. Add to mushrooms. Cook for 3 minutes, stirring occasionally.

⑥ Add wine. Cook and stir to loosen any flavorful browned bits to mix into the sauce. Stir in chicken broth, salt, pepper, and thyme.

⑦ Drain pasta. Stir into mushroom mixture. Continue simmering mixture until all moisture is absorbed, about 3 minutes.

⑧ Divide into four equal portions (each about 1¼ cups). Top each with 1 tablespoon shredded parmesan cheese.

14 Linguini with Clam Sauce

Ingredients

12 oz whole-wheat linguini

1 Tbsp olive oil

1 Tbsp garlic, minced (about 2–3 cloves)

1 Tbsp lemon juice

1 C low-sodium chicken broth

2 C canned whole clams, undrained

2 Tbsp fresh parsley, minced (or 2 tsp dried)

¼ tsp salt

¼ tsp ground black pepper

1 Tbsp butter

How to prepare

① In a 4-quart saucepan, bring 3 quarts of water to a boil over high heat.

② Add linguini, and cook according to package directions for the shortest recommended time, about 9 minutes.

③ Heat olive oil in a large saucepan. Add garlic, and cook gently until it begins to soften, about 30 seconds. Do not brown.

④ Add lemon juice and chicken broth. Bring to a boil. Add clams, along with liquid, parsley, salt, pepper, and butter. Simmer just until heated through, about 1–2 minutes. Do not overcook.

⑤ Strain the linguini, then add the pasta to the saucepan with the clams and mix well.

⑥ Divide into four equal portions (each about 2½ cups), and serve.

15 Lemon and Garlic Pasta with Pan-seared Scallops

Ingredients

1 large lemon, grated for zest (and freshly squeezed for 2 Tbsp lemon juice)

1 Tbsp garlic, minced or pressed (about 2–3 cloves)

2 Tbsp olive oil, divided into two 1-Tbsp portions

16 large sea scallops (about 1 lb)

¼ tsp salt

1/8 tsp ground black pepper

8 oz very thin spaghetti (vermicelli or angel hair)

2 Tbsp shredded parmesan cheese

How to prepare

① In a 4-quart saucepan, bring 3 quarts of water to a boil over high heat. When the water boils, reduce heat to simmer until you're ready to cook the pasta (step 5).

② While the water is heating up, use a grater to take off small peels of the skin of the lemon into a small saucepan. Cut the lemon in half and squeeze the juice into the pan and remove pits. Use the back of a large spoon to press the inside of the lemon to extract more juice. Add the garlic and 1 tablespoon of the olive oil to the saucepan. Stir to blend well. Place on stovetop on low heat.

③ Heat a large nonstick pan or grill pan on high temperature until very hot. Sprinkle the scallops with salt, pepper, and 1 tablespoon of olive oil. Toss to coat well.

④ Place the scallops in the hot pan. Cook about 4 minutes on each side, or until scallops are well browned and firm and milky white to the center (to a minimum internal temperature of 145 °F).

⑤ After turning the scallops to the second side, drop the pasta into the boiling water. Set temperature on medium, and cook for 2 minutes or the shortest recommended time according to package directions.

⑥ When the pasta is done, set aside ½ cup of the cooking water. Drain the pasta. Return drained pasta to the pot, and toss with the warm olive oil mixture and the ½ cup reserved pasta water.

⑦ Divide the pasta equally among four plates (about 1 cup per plate). Top each with four scallops.

⑧ Garnish each dish with ½ tablespoon of shredded parmesan cheese. Serve immediately.

16 Classic Macaroni and Cheese

Ingredients

2 C macaroni

½ C onion, chopped

½ C fat-free evaporated milk

1 medium egg, lightly beaten

¼ tsp ground black pepper

1¼ C (4 oz) low-fat sharp cheddar cheese, finely shredded

Cooking spray

How to prepare

① Cook macaroni according to package directions—but do not add salt to the cooking water. Drain and set aside.

② Spray a casserole dish with nonstick cooking spray.

③ Preheat oven to 350 °F.

④ Lightly spray a saucepan with nonstick cooking spray. Add onion to saucepan and sauté for about 3 minutes over medium heat.

⑤ In a bowl, combine macaroni, onion, and the remaining ingredients, and mix thoroughly. Transfer the mixture into casserole dish.

⑥ Bake for 25 minutes or until bubbly. Let stand for 10 minutes before serving.

17 Corn and Black Bean Burritos

Ingredients

¼ C scallions (green onions), rinsed and sliced into ¼-inch wide circles, including green tops

¼ C celery, rinsed and finely diced

1¼ C frozen yellow corn

½ ripe avocado, peeled and diced

2 Tbsp fresh cilantro, chopped (or substitute 2 tsp dried coriander)

1 can (15½ oz) black beans, drained and rinsed

¼ C reduced-fat shredded cheddar cheese

¼ C salsa or taco sauce (look for lowest sodium version)

12 (9-inch) whole-wheat tortillas

How to prepare

① Preheat oven to 350 °F.

② Combine scallions, celery, and corn in a small saucepan. Add just enough water to cover. Cover, bring to a boil, and reduce heat to medium. Simmer for 5 minutes, until vegetables soften. Drain vegetables. Set aside to cool.

③ Combine avocado, cilantro, and beans in a large mixing bowl. Add cheese and salsa, and mix.

④ When corn mixture has cooled slightly, add to avocado mixture.

⑤ In a large nonstick pan over medium heat, warm each tortilla for about 15 seconds on each side. Place each tortilla on a flat surface. Spoon 1/3 cup of the mixture into the center of the tortilla. Fold the top and bottom of the tortilla over the filling. Fold in the sides to make a closed packet.

⑥ Repeat with the remaining tortillas.

⑦ When all tortillas are wrapped, continue heating in the oven 5 minutes, until all are warm and cheese is melted.

18 Broccoli with Asian Tofu

Ingredients

1 pkg (16 oz) firm tofu, drained

2 Tbsp lite soy sauce

1 tsp sesame oil (optional)

½ Tbsp brown sugar

1 Tbsp fresh ginger root, finely chopped or shredded (or 1 tsp ground)

1 lb fresh broccoli, rinsed and cut into individual spears

1 Tbsp peanut oil or vegetable oil

¼ tsp crushed red pepper

4 Tbsp garlic, peeled and thinly sliced (about 8 cloves)

1 Tbsp sesame seeds (optional)

Cooking spray

How to prepare

① Slice tofu into eight pieces. Place on a plate or flat surface covered with three paper towels. Top with four more paper towels. Top with another flat plate or cutting board. Press down evenly and gently to squeeze out moisture. Throw away paper towels. Replace with fresh paper towels and press again. (The more liquid you remove, the more sauce the tofu will absorb.)

② Place tofu in a bowl just big enough to hold all eight pieces lying on their widest side without overlapping.

③ In a small bowl, combine the soy sauce, sesame oil, brown sugar, and ginger into a marinade, and stir thoroughly. Pour over tofu. Carefully turn the tofu several times to coat well. Set aside.

④ Meanwhile, heat a large nonstick sauté pan coated with cooking spray. Add broccoli and sauté for about 5 minutes, until it turns bright green and becomes tender and crispy. Remove broccoli from pan and set aside.

⑤ Heat a grill pan or flat sauté pan over high heat. Drain tofu, reserving marinade. Place on grill pan to heat for about 3 minutes. Gently turn. Heat the second side for 3 minutes.

⑥ At the same time, in the sauté pan over medium-low heat, warm the peanut oil, crushed red pepper, and garlic until the garlic softens and begins to turn brown, about 30 seconds to 1 minute. Add broccoli and reserved marinade, and gently mix until well-coated.

⑦ Place two slices of tofu on each plate with one-quarter of the broccoli and marinade mixture. Sprinkle with sesame seeds (optional).

REFERENCE
참고 문헌

Retrieved Jan. 10, 2019 from https://healthyeating.nhlbi.nih.gov/

Retrieved Jan. 10, 2019 from https://healthplans.providence.org/

“There is no sincere love than the love of food.”

- George Bernard Shaw (26 July 1856 - 2 November 1950), an Irish playwright, critic, polemicist and political activist

5
CHAPTER

Chinese Recipes

(Source: Ingredients of Wu Xiang Fen (Five spice powder) are Sichuan peppercorn, cloves, cinnamon, fennel seeds, and star anise., Retrieved 12 Feb 2019 from https://en.wikipedia.org/wiki/Chinese_cuisine#/media/File:Five_spices_detailed.jpg)

CHAPTER 5

Chinese Recipes

1 Chinese Chicken Salad

Ingredients

3/4 lb chicken breasts

2 tsps salt

2 tsps roasted sesame seeds

1/2 lb iceberg lettuce, finely shredded

2 tsps rice vinegar

Sauce:

1 garlic clove, minced

1 slice fresh peeled ginger

2 green onions, green top removed

2 tsps chili bean paste

2 tsps dark soy sauce

1 tsp sugar

2 tsps rice vinegar

2 tsps peanut butter

1/2 tsp salt

1/2 tsp ground black pepper

2 tsps toasted sesame oil

How to prepare

① Remove skin from the chicken breasts and place the chicken in a pot.

② Pour in enough cold water to cover the chicken and add the salt. Bring the mixture to a simmer and cook for 5 minutes. Turn off the heat and cover tightly, let it stand for 10 minutes.

③ Meanwhile, mix all the sauce ingredients and blend well.

④ Toss the lettuce with rice vinegar and place on a serving platter.

⑤ Remove the chicken from the pot and allow to cool. Pull the meat off the bone, shred it, and toss it with the sauce.

⑥ Place the chicken and sauce on top of the lettuce and serve at once.

2 Crispy Phoenix-tailed Shrimp

Ingredients

1 lb fresh raw shrimp

2 tsps light soy sauce

1 tsp rice wine

1 tsp five-spice powder

1/4 tsp freshly ground black pepper

2 cups cooking oil

1/2 cup cornstarch

2 eggs, beaten

2/3 cup bread crumbs

How to prepare

① Peel shrimp and discard the shells. Partially split the shrimp lengthways and remove the digestive cord. pat the shrimp dry with paper towels.

② Place the shrimp in a bowl and mix with the soy sauce, rice wine, five-spice powder and pepper.

③ Heat a wok and add the oil.

④ Dip the shrimp in the cornstarch, shaking them gently to remove any excess, then dip them into the beaten eggs, and finally coat the with the bread crumbs.

⑤ When the oil begins to smoke slightly, deep-fry the coated shrimp for 3 to 4 minutes, until golden brown. Drain them well on paper towels and serve at once.

3 Grilled Shrimp with Cilantro and Ginger Sauce

Ingredients

1 lb fresh raw shrimp

Marinade:

1 tsp light soy sauce

1 tsp rice wine

1 tsp sesame oil

Sauce:

2 tsps minced fresh cilantro

2 tsps white rice vinegar

1 tsp chopped peeled fresh ginger

How to prepare

① Preheat the broiler.

② Peel shrimp and discard the shells. Partially split the shrimp lengthways and remove the digestive cord. pat the shrimp dry with paper towels.

③ Combine the marinade ingredients, add shrimp and set aside for 10 minutes.

④ Prepare the sauce ingredients, mix them together and set aside.

⑤ Lay the shrimp on a baking tray, put on the lower tray in the oven. Cook the shrimp for 3 minutes on one side, turn over, and cook for 2 minutes.

⑥ Place on a serving platter and serve with sauce.

4 Beef with Oyster Sauce

Ingredients

3/4 lb lean boneless beef steak such as top round, flank, sirloin or New York steak

1 tsp dry sherry or cooking wine

1 tsp soy sauce

1 tsp water

1/4 tsp sugar

2 tsps cornstarch

3 1/2 tsps cooking oil

1 garlic, minced

1/2 tsp minced ginger

1/2 cup sliced bamboo shoots

6 medium dried Chinese mushrooms, thinly sliced

salt to taste

Cooking sauce:

2 tsps oyster sauce

1 tsp cornstarch

1/2 cup chicken broth

How to prepare

① Cut beef into 1/8-inch slices. Stir together cornstarch, soy sauce, dry sherry, sugar, and water. Add the beef and stir to coat. Then stir in 1 1/2 tsps of the oil and let marinate for 15 minutes.

② Prepare cooking sauce and set aside.

③ Heat a wok over high heat, add 2 tsps of the oil. Add ginger and garlic, stir once. Add beef and stir-fry until beef is brown, remove from wok and set aside.

④ Reheat wok with remaining 1 tsp of cooking oil, stir-fry bamboo shoots and mushrooms for 1 minute. Add 1 tsp water and stir-fry for 2 minutes.

⑤ Return beef to wok and stir in sauce mixture. Bring to a boil and thicken it.

⑥ Season to taste with salt and serve.

Note: bamboo shoots and mushroom can be substituted with 1 lb of asparagus.

5 Chinese Beef Stew

Ingredients

1 1/2 lbs stewing beef, cut into 1-inch cubes

2 tsps light soy sauce

1/2 cup all-purpose flour

1/4 cup cooking oil

10 cloves garlic, lightly smashed

4 slices fresh ginger

2 cups beef stock

1 cup water

2 star anise,

12 small carrots, trimmed and diced

12 small white onions, trimmed and peeled

How to prepare

① Cut beef into 1-inch cubes. Toss with the flour to coat. Shake off excess flour.

② Heat oil in a wok until hot, add as many beef as will fit and pan-fry to golden brown.

③ Repeat for all the beef. Remove and set aside.

④ Reheat the oil, stir-fry the garlic and ginger for 10 seconds, until fragrant.

⑤ Add the broth, water, soy sauce and star anise and heat until boiling.

⑥ Return the meat and bring back to a boil. Reduce heat, cover and simmer for 45 minutes. Add the carrots and onions, cook for another 45 minutes.

⑦ Skim any fat off the surface, and serve.

6 Spicy Stir-fried Hunan Beef

Ingredients

1 lb lean boneless beef steak such as top round, flank, sirloin or New York steak

Marinade:

2 tsps light soy sauce

1 tsp rice wine

2 tsps salt

2 tsps sesame oil

2 tsps cornstarch

3 tsps cooking oil

1 tsp minced fresh ginger

2 tsps garlic, minced

1 small onion, coarsely chopped

4 oz fresh red chilies, seeded and finely shredded

4 oz fresh green chilies, seeded and finely shredded

2 tsps coarsely chopped black beans

Cooking sauce:

3 tsps water

1 1/2 tsps rice wine or dry sherry

1 tsp light soy sauce

2 tsps sugar

2 tsps sesame oil

How to prepare

① Cut beef into 1/4-inch slides, then stack them and finely shred. Combine beef with the marinade mixture and mix well.

② Prepare cooking sauce and set aside.

③ Heat a wok over high heat, and add the oil. Add beef and brown for 1 minute over medium heat and then stir-fry for another minute. Drain the beef - leaving 1 tsp of oil.

④ Reheat the wok, add black beans, ginger and garlic and stir-fry for 20 seconds. Add chilies and stir-fry for another 20 seconds. Stir in the cooking sauce, cook over high heat for 30 seconds.

⑤ Return the beef to wok, add salt to taste. Give the mixture several stirs and mix well.

⑥ Turn onto serving platter and serve.

7 Braised Chicken and Mushroom

Ingredients

1 1/2 lbs chicken thighs

1 oz Chinese mushrooms

3 3/4 cups warm water

1 tsp cooking oil

1/2 lb yellow onions, sliced

2 tsps chopped peeled fresh ginger

1/4 cup oyster sauce

1 tsp sesame oil

How to prepare

① Remove the bones from the chicken thighs by running a knife through to the bone on each side, then cut out the bone. Remove the skin and cut the chicken into 1-inch cubes.

② Soak the mushrooms in the warm water for 20 minutes, or until soft. Squeeze the excess liquid from the mushrooms and remove the stalks. Cut the caps into quarters. Save the soaking liquid.

③ Heat a wok, add the cooking oil, and then the chicken. Stir-fry for 4 minutes, until the chicken begins to brown. Pour off excess fat.

④ Add the onions, ginger, garlic and mushrooms and stir-fry for 2 minutes. Then add oyster sauce and 2/3 cup of the soaking liquid. Continue cooking over high heat for 5 minutes, toss with sesame oil.

⑤ Serve at once.

8 Cantonese Lemon Chicken

Ingredients

1 lb boneless, skinless chicken breast halves, cut into 1-inch cubes

3 green onions, cut into thin slices

Batter:

1/3 cup all purpose flour

1/4 cup cornstarch

1/4 tsp salt

1/3 cup water

2 tsps cooking oil

Sauce:

1 cup water

2 tsps sugar

2 tsps lemon juice

4 tsps cornstarch

How to prepare

① Pat the chicken dry with paper towels.

② For batter, combine flour, cornstarch and salt. Add the water and 2 tsps of oil, beat until smooth.

③ Heat a wok with 2-inch of cooking oil to 365F.

④ Dip the chicken into the batter, swirling to coat. Allow the excess batter to drip off.

⑤ Fry the chicken, a few pieces at a time, for 4-5 minutes or till golden brown, turning once. Remove from the wok and drain on paper towels.

⑥ Arrange on a serving platter and keep warm in a 300F oven.

⑦ For sauce, combine all the ingredients, cook and stir in a saucepan until thicken and bubbly.

⑧ Add the sliced onions and stir to coat and cook for 2 minutes.

⑨ Drizzle the sauce over chicken and serve. Garnish with lemon slices.

9 General Tang's Chicken

Ingredients

1 lb boneless skinless chicken thighs, cut into 1-inch pieces

Marinade:

1 tsp salt

1/2 tsp black pepper

1 tsp light soy sauce

2 tsps rice wine

2 tsps cornstarch

1 tsp sesame oil

Batter:

2 tsps cornstarch

1/2 cup all-purpose flour

1 tsp baking powder

5 fl oz water

1/2 tsp salt

1 tsp cooking oil

1 tsp sesame oil

Sauce:

1 1/2 tsps cooking oil

5 dried red chilies, seeded, halved

5 garlic cloves, sliced

2 tsps vinegar

3 tsps sugar

1 tsp salt

1 cup water

1 tsp cornstarch in 1 tsp water

Cooking oil for deep-frying

How to prepare

① Combine the chicken with the marinade ingredients, mix well. Let marinate for 20 minutes.

② Mix the batter ingredients until smooth. Combine the batter with the chicken.

③ Heat a wok with the oil. Stir-fry the garlic and chilies until fragrant, add the rest of sauce ingredients, simmer uncovered for 10 minutes.

④ Heat a wok over high heat until hot, then add oil for deep-frying.

⑤ When oil is hot, deep-fry the chicken, a few at a time until golden and crispy. ⑤ Drain well on paper towels and set on a warm platter, pour the sauce over chicken and serve.

10 Fried Crab in Balck Bean Sauce

Ingredients

1 medium crab, cleaned and crushed

1 tsp salted black bean

1 large garlic clove, crushed

1 tsp soy sauce

1 tsp sugar

4 tsps cooking oil

1 garlic clove, cut into two

2 slices fresh ginger

8 tsps hot water

2 tsps cornstarch in 1 tsp cold water

3 shallots, chopped

1 egg, slightly beaten

How to prepare

① Cut crab body into quarters, leave legs and claws whole, set aside.

② Rinse the black beans with cold water and drain. Mash beans well and mix with the crushed garlic, soy sauce and sugar.

③ Heat oil in a wok, fry the halved garlic clove, shallots and ginger slices until they start to brown, remove from the wok.

④ Over high heat, fry the pieces of crab, stir and turn constantly for 4-5 minutes, until shells are bright red. Remove crab from the wok.

⑤ Add black bean mixture to the oil and fry for 1 minute, then add hot water and crab pieces, cook for 3 minutes.

⑥ Stir in cornstarch mixture, bring to a boil and thicken it. Add egg, stir until egg sets.

11 Almond Jelly with Melon

Ingredients

2 1/2 tsps unflavored gelatin

1 cups warm water

2 tsps sugar

1/2 cup condensed milk

1 1/2 tsps almond extract

2 cups ripe melon or cantaloupe, cut into balls or 1-inch diamonds

How to prepare

① Place a 8 or 9-inch square or round cake pan in the freezer to chill.

② Sprinkle the gelatin over 1/2 cup of water in a small saucepan and let sit until softened, for about 5 minutes. Then heat the mixture over low heat until boiling, stir constantly until the gelatin dissolves. Remove from the heat.

③ Combine sugar and remaining 1/2 cups water, condensed milk and almond extract in a bowl and stir to dissolve the sugar. Stir in the dissolved gelatin.

④ Pour into the chilled pan and refrigerate until set (about 4 hours). Cut the chilled almond jelly into 1-inch diamond-shaped pieces.

⑤ Place the almond jelly and melon in serving bowls and serve.

12 Apple-Blueberry Delight

Ingredients

2 tsps sugar

1 tsp ground cinnamon

1/4 tsp ground nutmeg

2 large orange, juice and grated peel

4 tart green apples

2 tsps butter or margarine

1 pint blueberries

Whipped cream

How to prepare

① Mix sugar, cinnamon and nutmeg in a bowl, set aside.

② Peel, core and thinly slice the apples.

③ In a large bowl, mix orange juice and peel, add the apple slices and toss well.

④ Heat a wok with the butter, when butter melts, add the sugar mixture and cook for about a minute.

⑤ Add the apple mixture and stir-fry until apples are soft (about 3 minutes).

⑥ Add blueberries, stir-fry until sauce is thickened.

⑦ Transfer to dessert plates, serve with whipped cream on top.

13 Baked Fish Packages

Ingredients

8 thin trout fillets, skin removed

8 twelve-inch squares aluminum foil

Marinade:

2 tsps rice wine

3 slices fresh ginger, smashed

1 tsp cooking oil

Sauce:

1 cup chicken broth

2 tsps light soy sauce

2 tsps rice wine or sake

1 tsp sugar

1 tsp cornstarch in 1 tsp water

Seasonings:

1/2 cup finely shredded green onions

1/4 cup finely shredded fresh ginger

1/4 cup finely shredded shiitake mushrooms

How to prepare

① Wash and dry the fish fillets, put in a bowl. Combine the marinade ingredients and slightly pinch the ginger slices in the rice wine to impart their flavor.

② Add to the fillets and toss lightly to coat. Chill for 20 minutes.

③ Combine the sauce ingredients and blend well.

④ Preheat oven to 450F.

⑤ Heat a wok, add the oil, and heat until very hot. Add the seasonings and stir fry for 15 seconds. Add the sauce mixture and bring to a boil, stir until thickened.

⑥ Remove from the heat and let cool slightly.

⑦ Arrange 1 fillet on each foil, spoon the sauce mixture over the fish and fold the foil over to enclose the fish completely. Fold and crimp the edged of the packages to seal.

⑧ Arrange the packages on a cookies sheet and bake for 8 minutes, or until the packages puff up. Serve immediately.

14 Curried Fish

Ingredients

1 lb fresh or frozen swordfish, shark, sea bass, tuna or monkfish

1/2 cup water

2 tsps hoisin sauce

1 tsp curry powder or paste

1/2 tsp sugar

1 tsp cooking oil

1 cup carrots, cut into strips

1 cup celery, cut into strips

1 can (8oz) bamboo shoots, drained and cut into strips

How to prepare

① Cut fish into 1-inch cubes, discard bone and skin.

② Combine water, hoisin sauce, curry powder, and sugar.

③ Pour oil into a wok, heat over medium-high heat. Add carrots and celery, stir fry for 3 minutes. Add bamboo shoots, stir-fry for 1 minute.

④ Remove. Add half of the fish to the hot wok, stir-fry for 3-6 minutes, until fish flakes easily. Remove. Repeat with remaining fish.

⑤ Stir sauce mix, add to the wok. Cook and stir until slightly thickened.

⑥ Return vegetables and fish to wok. Stir well and simmer for 2 minutes.

⑦ Serve immediately.

15 Steamed Salmon with Black Bean Sauce

Ingredients

1 lb fresh salmon fillets, slice into 1-inch-thick

1 tsp salt

2 tsps toasted sesame oil

Sauce:

1 tsp cooking oil

2 tsps coarsely chopped salted black beans

1 1/2 tsps garlic, minced

1 tsp finely chopped peeled fresh ginger

3 tsps coarsely chopped green onions

1 tsp dark soy sauce

2 tsps light soy sauce

2/3 cup water

1 tsp cornstarch mixed with 1 tsp water

How to prepare

① Set a rack into a wok. Add in water to a depth of 2 1/2-inches and bring it to a simmer.

② Rub the salmon fillets with salt and toasted sesame oil and place on a heatproof plate that will fit into the wok.

③ Place the plate holding the fish on the rack, cover tightly and steam for 6 minute.

④ Meanwhile, heat a wok then add oil, black beans, garlic, and ginger. Stir-fry for 1 minute, then add the green onions, soy sauces and water, simmer for 1 minute. Add the cornstarch mixture and stir until thickened.

⑤ When the salmon is cooked, pour the hot sauce over the salmon and serve at once.

16 Chinese Lamb Stew

Ingredients

2 1/2 lbs lamb leg or shoulder meat,

2 tsps cooking oil

1/2 tsp ground pepper

6 garlic cloves, crushed

6 slices fresh ginger

5 cups water

2 tsps five-spice powder

1/3 cup peanut butter

6 tsps hoisin sauce

3 tsps light soy sauce

3 tsps dark soy sauce

1/4 cup granulated sugar

1 tsp chili bean paste

How to prepare

① Cut the lamb into 1-inch cubes.

② Heat a wok and add the oil. Add the lamb, sprinkle with the pepper, and slowly brown on all sides. Transfer the meat to a pot. Pour in all but 1 tsp of oil from the wok.

③ Reheat the wok, stir-fry ginger and garlic for 20 seconds and add the rest of the ingredients. Bring the mixture to a boil and pour it over the lamb in the pot.

④ Simmer for 1 1/2 hour, until lamb is tender.

17 Shrimp Chow Mein

Ingredients

1/2 lb dried egg noodles

1 lb shelled cooked shrimp

2 eggs, beaten

2 tsps cooking oil

1 medium onion, sliced

10 water chestnuts, sliced

6 dried Chinese mushrooms, soaked, sliced

1/2 cup water

1 1/3 cups Napa cabbage

1/2 tsp salt

1/2 tsp instant chicken bouillon granules

1 tsp cornstarch in 1 tsp water

2 green onions, chopped

How to prepare

① Boil the egg noodles in boiling salted water, follow the instructions on the package. Drain and keep warm.

② Heat a wok with lightly oiled, pour the eggs into wok and swirl to spread the egg. Turn once when egg is set. Remove from the wok and let it cool.

③ Thinly slice the egg omelette and set aside.

④ Heat a wok with the oil, sti-fry the onion, water chestnuts, and mushrooms for 3 minutes. Add napa cabbage, salt, instant chicken bouillon and water, cover and cook for 3 minutes. Add shrimp and cornstarch mixture, bring to a boil and simmer until thickened.

⑤ Place noodles in a warm serving platter, top with vegetable and shrimp mixture.

⑥ Garnish with the egg slices and green onions. Serve warm.

18 Barbecued Pork

Ingredients

1 lb pork belly or fillet

3 garlic cloves

1/2 tsp finely grated ginger

1 tsp salt

1 tsp dark soy sauce

1 tsp honey

1 tsp rice wine

1/2 tsp five-spice powder

How to prepare

① Cut the meat lengthwise into strips about 1-inch wide. Crush garlic with salt and combine with all other ingredients in a large bowl. Put in the pork, mix well together to coat the pork with the marinade. Marinate for 15 minutes or longer.

② Preheat oven at 425F.

③ Half fill a roasting pan with hot water and place a wire rack across the top of the pan.

④ Place the pork on the rack and roast in hot oven for 30 minutes.

⑤ Turn the pork over, brush with the remaining marinade and roast for further 15 minutes or until well glazed.

⑥ Cut into slices and serve. Use hoisin sauce or plum sauce for dipping.

참고 문헌

REFERENCE

Retrieved Jan. 15, 2019 from https://www.geniuskitchen.com/
Retrieved Jan. 15, 2019 from https://www.cookstr.com
Retrieved Jan. 15, 2019 from https://www.chinahighlights.com/
Retrieved Jan. 15, 2019 from www.eatingwell.com/
Retrieved Jan. 15, 2019 from https://rasamalaysia.com/
Retrieved Jan. 16, 2019 from https://www.jessicagavin.com/
Retrieved Jan. 16, 2019 from https://thewoksoflife.com/
Retrieved Jan. 16, 2019 from https://www.delish.com/
Retrieved Jan. 16, 2019 from https://www.allrecipes.com/
Retrieved Jan. 16, 2019 from https://www.bbcgoodfood.com/
Retrieved Jan. 16, 2019 from https://www.realsimple.com/
Retrieved Jan. 15, 2019 from http://messywitchen.com/recipe/
Retrieved Jan. 15, 2019 from https://www.coffeecatskimchi.com/

"One cannot think well, love well, sleep well, if one has not dined well."

- Virginia Woolf (25 January 1882 - 28 March 1941), an English writer

6
CHAPTER

Japanese Recipes

(Source: Soba noodles, Retrieved 2 Feb 2019 from https://en.wikipedia.org/wiki/Japanese_cuisine#/media/File:Otsu_Tsuruki-soba01st3200.jpg)

CHAPTER

6 Japanese Recipes

1 Tazukuri (soy sauce sugar-glazed sardines)

Ingredients

2 ounces gomame (dried baby sardines)

1/3 cup dashi (or water)

1/3 cup soy sauce

3 1/2 tablespoons granulated sugar

1 tablespoon mirin

1 takanotsume (Japanese “hawk claw” pepper) (or substitute 1 dried red chile pepper)

How to prepare

① Pick out any broken fish. To pan toast: Cook the fish in a dry pan over medium-low heat until fragrant, lightly toasted, and crispy (about 3 minutes). To microwave toast: Spread the fish in a circle on a plate lined with a paper towel and microwave on high for 2.5 minutes, making sure the fish don't burn.

② Mix the dashi, soy sauce, sugar, mirin, and takanotsume together in a small saucepan and bring to a boil. Then add the toasted fish and simmer for a couple of minutes until the mixture has reduced and is thick and syrupy.

③ Spread the fish out on a large plate to cool.

2 Yaki Shiitake (shiitake & scallion yakitori)

Ingredients

For the tare (basting sauce):

½ cup soy sauce

½ cup mirin

¼ granulated sugar

For the skewers:

16 large fresh shiitake mushrooms, preferably donko

1 bunch scallions

Vegetable oil

How to prepare

① Make the tare: Put the soy sauce, mirin, and sugar into a small saucepan and cook over medium-low heat. When the mixture begins to boil, reduce the heat to low, and continue cooking over low heat for 20 minutes. Skim any scum off the surface as the sauce is cooking. Set aside.

② Make the skewers: Soak the bamboo skewers in water for 20 minutes. Preheat the grill. Clean the mushrooms with a slightly damp paper towel or cotton cloth, then cut away and discard the stems. Cut the firm white and whitish green parts of the scallions into 1 ¾ inch lengths.

③ Thread two mushrooms (lengthwise through the mushroom caps) and two pieces of scallion onto each skewer, alternating between the mushrooms and scallion pieces. Brush the mushrooms and scallions with a light layer of vegetable oil.

④ Place the skewers on the grill, with mushrooms facing gill side up. Cook the skewers until the tops of the mushroom caps are dry. Turn the skewers over (mushrooms gill side down), and cook them until the insides become wet with the mushrooms' own juice. Turn the skewers over (mushrooms gill side up) one more time and cook for about 1 or 2 minutes more until the mushrooms and scallions are completely cooked through.

⑤ Remove the skewers from the grill, and with a pastry brush, baste them with the tare. Arrange the skewers on a large plate and serve.

3 Dashi Stock (出汁, だし)

Dashi is a class of soup and cooking stock, considered fundamental to Japanese cooking. Dashi forms the base for miso soup, clear broth, noodle broth, and many kinds of simmering liquid. The most common form of dashi is a simple broth or stock made by heating water containing kombu (edible kelp) and kezurikatsuo (shavings of katsuobushi – preserved, fermented tuna) to near-boiling, then straining the resultant liquid.

Fresh dashi, made from dried kelp and katsuobushi, is rare today, even in Japan. Most people now use granulated or liquid instant substitutes.

Other kinds of dashi stock are made by soaking kelp, niboshi, or shiitake in water for many hours or by heating them in near-boiling water and straining the resulting broth.

Kombu dashi stock is made by soaking kelp in water. Niboshi dashi stock is made by pinching off the heads and entrails of small dried sardines, to prevent bitterness, and soaking the remains in water. Shiitake dashi stock is made by soaking dried shiitake mushrooms in water.

1) Ichiban Dashi (first sea stock)

Ingredients

4 cups water

16-20 square inches of kombu*

1/2 cup loosely packed katsuobushi

How to prepare

① Place the water and the kombu in a pot and let the kombu soak for about 15 minutes. Place the pot over medium heat. Right before the water starts to boil (watch for bubbles starting to break around the edge of the pot), remove the pot from the heat and scatter the katsuobushi over the surface of the water.

② After 3 or 4 minutes (the katsuobushi will have sunk to the bottom of the pot by this point), strain the stock through a strainer lined with a tightly woven cotton cloth or a coffee-filter.

③ Refrigerate the stock in a tightly covered container for up to 4 days in the refrigerator.**

* If you would like to weigh out your kombu (I usually eyeball it)-somewhere between 0.45-ounces or 0.6 ounces (13-18 grams) is good! Of course, you can always go with more or less depending on your tastes.

** Sources disagree on whether ichiban dashi can be frozen. Some say that it can be frozen, while others argue that the stock loses its aroma/flavor when frozen, so it's best to use it when it's fresh. It's up to you!

2) Niban Dashi (second sea stock)

Ingredients

4 cups water

Kombu and katsuobushi used in ichiban dashi

How to prepare

① Combine all of the ingredients in a pot. Place the pot over low heat and cook the mixture for 10 minutes. Remove the pot from the heat and then strain the stock through a strainer lined with tightly woven cotton cloth or a coffee-filter.

② Refrigerate the stock in a tightly covered container for up to 4 days in the refrigerator.

3) Niboshi dashi is a Japanese fish stock made from dried sardines. It's often used to make miso soup in Japan.

Ingredients

2/3 oz niboshi (dried sardines)

4 and 1/4 cup water

How to prepare

① Remove the heads of niboshi and tear niboshi in halves and gut them.

② Put water in a deep pot and soak niboshi for one hour or more. Bring it to a boil and simmer on low heat for about 5 minutes, skimming off any foam rise to the surface. Stop the heat.

③ Place a paper towel in a colander and strain the stock through it..

4 Sashimi (さしみ, 刺身, sliced raw fish)

Sashimi is a Japanese delicacy primarily consisting of very fresh raw seafood, sliced into thin pieces and served with only a dipping sauce (soy sauce with wasabi paste and thinly-sliced ginger root or ponzu), and a simple garnish such as shiso and shredded daikon radish.

Japanese Assorted Sashimi with Soy Dip Recipe

Ingredients

8 fresh medium shrimp

1/4 pound freshly shucked scallops

5 ounces fresh tuna fillet

5 ounces fresh salmon fillet

5 ounces fresh mackerel or snapper fillet

1/2 teaspoon oil

8 ounces daikon radish (about 4 inches), grated into long thin shreds

4 shiso leaves

4 teaspoons wasabi paste

Sashimi Soy Dip (see recipe below), to serve

How to prepare

① Prepare the Sashimi Soy Dip and set aside.

② Peel and clean the shrimp, but leave the head and tail on for a more authentic appearance.

③ Clean and dry the scallops. Heat the oil in a pan until moderately hot and sear the scallops for 30 seconds on each side. Remove from the heat and set aside.

④ Slice the tuna and salmon fillets on the diagonal into strips about 1/2 inch wide and 1 1/2 inches long.

⑤ The mackerel or snapper can either be sliced paper-thin or cut into decorative shapes.

⑥ Arrange the shrimp, scallops and cut fish on a serving platter.

⑦ Garnish with the daikon, shiso leaves and wasabi paste.

⑧ Serve the Assorted Sashimi with small bowls of Sashimi Soy Dip.

Sashimi Soy Dip Recipe*

Ingredients for Sashimi Soy Dip

3 tablespoons sake

1/2 cup Japanese soy sauce

2 tablespoons tamari soy sauce or mirin (sweet rice wine)

1/2 cup dried bonito flakes

1 small strip dried kelp (konbu), wiped with a damp cloth (optional)

How to prepare

① To make the Sashimi Soy Dip, place all the ingredients in a small saucepan and simmer on medium-low heat for 5 minutes.

② Remove from the heat, allow to cool, strain and discard solids.

* The Sashimi Soy Dip can be stored for up to a year if kept refrigerated in an airtight jar.

5 Grilled Spanish Mackerel

Ingredients

6 large Spanish mackerel fillets

1/4 cup olive oil

3 lemons, sliced

Salt and ground pepper to taste

How to prepare

① Light grill and set it to medium heat, cover the surface of the grill with aluminum foil.

② Rub both sides of the Spanish mackerel fillets with olive oil and place them skin side down onto the aluminum foil.

③ Sprinkle the spanish mackerel fillets with salt and pepper, cover each completely with the lemon slices.

④ Grill until meat just begins to flake, do not flip fillets.

⑤ Serve the Grilled Spanish Mackerel immediately.

6 Japanese Seafood Tempura

Serves/Makes: 6 servings as a main course or 10 to 12 servings as an hors d'oeuvre

Ingredients

1/2 pound large fresh shrimps

1 pound sea scallops

6 large parsley sprigs

1/2 small eggplant, cut in 2x1/4-inch strips

3/4 pound sweet potatoes, peeled and sliced 1/8-inch thick

1 large green pepper, sliced lengthwise in 1/4-inch strips

1/2 pound small fresh mushrooms

Oil, for deep frying

For batter:

1 egg yolk

2 cups ice-cold water

1/8 teaspoon baking soda

1 2/3 cups unsifted all-purpose flour

How to prepare

① Shell and devein shrimp, leaving tail on very tip of tail. Drop shrimp into boiling salted water to cover; bring back to a boil. Reduce heat, simmer, covered, 5 minutes. Drain; cool. Drop scallops into boiling salted water; bring back to a boil. Reduce heat, simmer, covered, 3 minutes. Drain; cool.

② On a large serving platter, arrange shrimp and scallops in an attractive pattern, with parsley, eggplant, sweet potato, green pepper, and whole mushrooms. Refrigerate, covered, until ready to cook.

③ MAKE BATTER – In a large mixing bowl, with a wooden spoon, combine the egg yolk with the ice-cold water and baking soda. With a wire whisk, stir in the unsifted flour to make a smooth batter; it will be thin. Use the batter soon after it is made; it should not stand.

④ In a deep fryer or heavy skillet, heat oil, at least 3-inches deep, to 375°F (180°C) on deep frying thermometer. With tongs, dip shrimp, scallops, and vegetables, one by one, into batter to coat lightly. Deep fry, a few at a time, until lightly browned – about 3 minutes.

⑤ Tempura is best served immediately with grated radish, horseradish, ginger root, and Tempura Dipping Sauce.

Tempura Dipping Sauce Recipe

Ingredients

1/2 cup sherry

1/2 cup beef broth

1 cup shoyu or soy sauce

Radishes, freshly grated

Horseradish, freshly grated

Ginger root, freshly grated

How to prepare

① In a small saucepan, combine sherry, beef broth, and shoyu or soy sauce; bring to a boil.

② Divide into 6 individual bowls.

③ Place on a tray with 3 small bowls filled with grated radish, horseradish, and ginger root.

7 Japanese Simmered Pork Shoulder

Ingredients

2 pound well-marbled pork shoulder roast, tied with kitchen twine (optional)*

2 leeks, rinsed well and sliced in half lengthwise

3 inches fresh ginger, peeled and sliced into 1/4-inch coins

7 fluid ounces soy sauce

7 fluid ounces mirin

7 fluid ounces honey

8 hard-boiled eggs, peeled, optional

Scallions, thinly sliced into matchsticks, for garnish

How to prepare

① Place the pork roast in a large pot, along with the halved leeks and sliced ginger. Add enough water to cover the pork by 1 to 2 inches, making note of where the water reaches in the pot. Bring the water to a simmer over medium heat, then reduce the heat to low to maintain a simmer. If you have an otoshi-buta place it on the pork, or if you don't, place the lid of the pot slightly askew, and swirl the pot occasionally in circular motions to help ensure even cooking.

② Let the pork simmer for two hours, skimming off any scum or foam that accumulates on the surface of the water or along the sides of the pot.

③ After two hours, take the pot off the heat, remove the otoshi-buta if you're using one, and let it cool until it's warm, then put the pot in the refrigerator to chill overnight.

④ The next day, skim the layer of fat off the top of the water, then remove the ginger and leeks. Return the pot to the stove, and bring the liquid to a simmer over medium heat. Continue cooking at a simmer until the broth is reduced to approximately half the amount of water that you started with.

⑤ Reduce the temperature to low, then add the soy sauce, mirin, and honey and stir to combine. Continue to cook for 15 minutes on low heat, then flip the meat over to cook the other side and cook for an additional 10 minutes. Remove the pot from the heat, put the pot lid on, then let the meat cool completely. Once the pork has cooled, it can be cut into thin slices and served with thinly sliced scallions, as desired. If you want to make shoyu tamago (soy sauce eggs), continue with step 6.

⑥ When the liquid is still warm, but no longer hot, add the peeled hard-boiled eggs to the liquid, then place the pot in the refrigerator overnight, with the lid on. The meat and eggs are ready to serve the following day. Remove the eggs and set them aside. Gently reheat the pork on the stove over medium-low heat. Thinly slice the meat and serve it with the shoyu tamago, sliced in halve, along with thinly sliced scallions.

8 Simmered Red Sea Bream

Ingredients

500g / 18oz red sea bream fillet

1/2 cup / 100ml sake

1/2 cup /100ml mirin (a sweet cooking sake)

5 tbsp soy sauce

1/4 cup / 50ml water

3 tbsp sugar

1 knob of ginger / 30g / 1oz – peeled and thinly sliced

How to prepare

① Cut the fillet into 4 pieces.

② Heat the sake, water, mirin and soy sauce in a pan. When the broth gets warm, add the sugar and dissolve it. When the broth comes to a boil, add the fillets. Put the fillets skin-side down in the pan to prevent the skin from shrinking.

③ Add the sliced ginger to the pan. Put the drop lid on and simmer for a few minutes.

④ When the skin side of the fillet is well cooked, turn it over. Continue cooking the fillets until half of the liquid is gone.

⑤ Turn off the heat and let it stand for a while, so the fish can absorb the extra liquid.

9 Chawan Mushi

Ingredients (makes small 6 cups):

2 large eggs

300 ml dashi stock

½ tsp soy sauce

½ tsp mirin

1/8 tsp salt

1 Tbsp sake

3 shiitake mushrooms, sliced

herb: mitsuba, daikon sprouts, or shiso, etc

Other optional suggestions: kamaboko, wakame, shrimp, chicken breast, yuzu peel, fu (wheat gluten), carrots, ginkgo nuts, etc.

How to prepare

① Stir the eggs in a bowl (try not to create bubbles too much). Add dashi, soy sauce, mirin, salt and sake, and continue to stir, gently.

② Run the egg mixture through strainer or cheese cloth and set aside.

③ Divide ingredients into prepared cups. Slowly pour egg mixture into the cups evenly.

④ Steam chawanmushi for about 10 minutes or until the egg mixture becomes opaque and solid. (If you are not using a steamer, you can fill a couple of inches of water in a large pot, place them gently, cover the pot with a lid and steam them over medium heat. The water should be simmering and never let it boil.) Remove from the heat. Serve warm.

10 Japanese Cucumber Salad (Sunomono)

Ingredients

2 to 3 Japanese cucumbers (you could use 1 large English cucumber a a substitute)

1 teaspoon salt

2 tablespoons rice wine vinegar

1 tablespoon sugar

1 drop soy sauce

How to prepare

① Peel and slice cucumbers into very thin slices. Sprinkle sliced cucumber slices with salt and let stand a few minutes. Squeeze out excess moisture.

② Combine the vinegar, sugar, and soy sauce in a bowl and mix well. Pour the vinegar mixture over the cucumber slices and mix well. Set aside for at least 15 minutes before serving.

③ Serve in individual dishes. I sometimes like to add daikon radish (peel and slice it into thin slices) or wakame (a delicious nutrient rich type of edible kelp). You can also add shrimp or crab meat if you want to add some protein.

Cook's Note

This also makes a great healthy addition to a bento.

11 Ball-shaped Sushi (salmon temarizushi)

Ingredients

5 ounces sushi-fresh salmon, sliced into thin squares (1 to 2 inches square)

2 tablespoons wasabi

2 cups sushi rice

2 1/2 tablespoons mayonnaise

1 bunch of chives, chopped into 1/2-inch pieces

How to prepare

① Lay a large square of plastic wrap on a clean dry work surface. Place a slice of salmon in the middle of the square. Put a tiny dot of wasabi in the middle of the salmon.

② With slightly damp hands, shape approximately 2 teaspoons of sushi rice into a ball and place the ball on top of the salmon.

③ Gather the plastic wrap up around the rice ball, then twist the plastic wrap, sealing the rice inside, and firmly press the rice into a ball shape (don't press too hard or you'll turn everything into rice mash).

④ While holding the plastic wrapped ball in one hand, use your forefinger of your free hand to gently press into the center of the salmon to make a small depression, flattening the rice ball slightly in the process.

⑤ Unwrap the ball and set it on a plate. Place a small drop of mayonnaise in the depression and garnish with several chive pieces.

⑥ Repeat the process with the rest of the ingredients.

Cook's Note

Don't be tempted to use more rice! Not only are smaller balls easier to eat, but one of the things that make temarizushi so delicious is the higher fish to rice ratio.

12 Anko Nabe

Ingredients

18 oz chopped anko (goosefish)

1/4 Chinese cabbage

6 shiitake mushrooms (marked with X's on top)

5 oz thick carrots

4 oz shimeji mushrooms

4 oz maitake mushrooms

1 shiro negi or two green onions (cut into 2.5″ pieces)

Spices

5 oz miso paste

1 slice of konbu

1/4 cup cooking sake

How to prepare

① Put 6 cups of water into a large pot or slow cooker (nabe). Add konbu and let sit for 20 mins at room temperature. Remove konbu.

② Add sake and anko (goosefish) and heat on high until mixture boils. Skim the top of the soup

③ Reduce heat to medium, then add miso paste and mix

④ Add remaining ingredients, cover, and boil for 5-10 minutes (until cooked).

⑤ Sample the soup and add miso to taste.

13 Nabeyaki Udon

Ingredients

6 ounces fresh spinach leaves

6 cups dashi (basic Japanese sea stock)

1/3 cup soy sauce

3 tablespoons mirin

1 teaspoon salt

3 cloves garlic, minced

1 tablespoon finely grated ginger

2 large carrots, peeled and thinly sliced on the diagonal

2 leeks, cleaned and cut into 1-inch slices on the diagonal

1 pound boneless, skinless chicken thighs

21 ounces fresh udon noodles

5 large eggs

How to prepare

① Bring a large pot of water to a rolling boil and cook the spinach for one minute. Quickly drain the spinach and plunge it into a bowl of cold water. Rinse with cold water until the spinach is completely cold. Squeeze out the water, then cut into 1-inch lengths. Set aside.

② Mix the dashi, soy sauce, mirin, and salt together in a 4-quart saucepan, then stir in the garlic and ginger. Add the sliced carrots and leeks, then bring the liquid to a boil over medium heat.

③ Add the chicken and simmer until just cooked through, about 5 minutes.

④ Add the udon noodles and place the spinach in 5 small bundles on the top. Simmer for 3 minutes.

⑤ Gently crack the eggs, one at a time, into the soup. Cover the pot with a lid, and let simmer for 3 minutes, then turn off the heat and let sit to allow the eggs to finish cooking.

14 Pickled Cabbage and Carrot (kyabetsu to ninjin no asazuke)

Ingredients

1 small head of regular cabbage (3/4 pound), the leaves cut into pieces about an inch square

1 medium sized carrot, cut into matchstick slices about an inch long

1 Japanese cucumber, unpeeled and cut into matchstick slices about an inch long

4 tablespoons of salt

How to prepare

① Place vegetable slices into the pickle press (or jar) and add one tablespoon of salt, mix well by stirring with your hands. Add the second tablespoon of salt and mix again. Add the final tablespoon of salt and mix well.

② Clamp on the top of the pickle press and screw down the lid until it pushes down tightly the top layer of vegetables.

③ Leave under pressure overnight or for at least 10 hours.

④ Remove the pickles from the press and place them in a colander, wash them well to remove salt, pat them dry and serve.

REFERENCE 참고문헌

Retrieved Jan. 16, 2019 from https://en.wikipedia.org/wiki/Dashi

Retrieved Jan. 16, 2019 from https://www3.nhk.or.jp/nhkworld/en/

Retrieved Jan. 17, 2019 from http://www.japanfoodaddict.com/

Retrieved Jan. 17, 2019 from https://www.lafujimama.com/

Retrieved Jan. 17, 2019 from http://www.theblackmoon.com/

"Be strong because things will get better. It may be stormy now, but it never rains forever."

- Unknown

7 CHAPTER

Expressions Among Kitchen Staff Members

(Source: Kitchen interior, cirka 1565, Retrieved 23 Jan 2019 from https://en.wikipedia.org/wiki/Kitchen#/media/File:M%C3%A5leri,_genrebild,_K%C3%B6ksinteri%C3%B6r_-_Skoklosters_slott_-_88962.tif)

CHAPTER 7

Expressions Among Kitchen Staff Members

1 Declarative Sentence

- Dishes are ready.
- It's very spicy.
- It's on the counter/on the island.
- (It's) In the island.
- (It's) In the drawer next to the sink.
- It's next to the dishwasher.
- It's to the right of the island.
- It's across from the dishwasher.
- It's above the refrigerator.
- It's under the sink.
- It's in the cabinet under the sink.
- (It's) In the middle drawer on the island.
- (It's) On the top shelf of the cabinet to the left of the stove.
- They are on top of the refrigerator.
- Cleaning products belong in the cupboard under the sink.

- Bottles of sesame oil and pine nuts go in the cupboard over the sink.
- Jane, it's your turn to do the dishes.
- My kitchen sink is clogged!
- My kitchen sink is clogged up again.
- It's clogged with hair.
- It's clogged and the water won't go down.
- My water faucet is dripping badly now.
- The broom and mop are standing in the closet.
- The dustpan is in there, too, hanging on a hook.
- The beef is in the oven.
- The ingredients are 1 cucumber, peeled and chopped, 2 fresh tomatoes, chopped, 2 green onion, minced, 1 red bell pepper, chopped and 5 radishes, chopped.
- I am chopping the vegetables.
- I am extracting the juice from mangoes/onions.
- I am doing the dishes.
- I'm preparing the fillets.
- I'm washing those dishes right now.
- I am kneading the dough.
- I am peeling the pumpkin.
- She was rolling out the flour.
- I was kneading the flour.
- I was sieving the flour.
- Kwangsu's boiling the broth and slicing the radish.
- I'm afraid the meat is rotten.
- There's a little rice left in that container.
- There are a few carrots on the counter.

- There are three cupboards above the sink.
- Vegetable is cooked now.
- It's not cooked.
- Potatoes are not cooked yet in the dish.
- The dessert was made with whipped cream.
- Jenkins gave us this recipe.
- I have my grandmother's recipe.
- I have the dough rolled out.
- I forgot to put it in the refrigerator.
- I thought we were all out of beef.
- He tossed the noodles.
- She mashed the potatoes.
- She knows how to knead the flour.
- I know how to bake the beef.
- We need an extra chair.
- I need the mixer to blend the cake ingredients.
- We need five tangpyeongchae and two dishes of hobak seon.
- We need flour, butter, salt, eggs, sugar, yeast and water, for the dough.
- We need to order more eggs.
- We need to prepare a half-pan of cucumbers and a batch of beef short ribs.
- we need to prepare a tray of beef and cut forty chickens.
- We need to prepare a tub of mung bean sprouts and a pan of lettuce.
- First you fry the onion.
- First you chop the garlic.
- First you blanch the soaked brown seaweed.
- Then you add salt and eggs.

- Then you fry it on a low heat until it is golden/brown.
- Minsu has just taken the pork out of the oven.
- I’ve got the ingredients on the table.
- I have picked out the rice.
- She has chopped the vegetables.
- She has peeled the green peas.
- She has sieved the flour.
- I’ve never made them before.
- I’ve already prepared the vegetables.
- I have to put the groceries away.
- I have to scour the large pan.
- I have to finish these orders first.
- I have to sweep and mop the kitchen floor.
- You have to slice the onion.
- You have to use very fresh yellowtail.
- You have to cook each ingredient separately.
- You have to stir it continually.
- You have to put ice in the bowl.
- You have to use very warm water.
- I'll wash the dishes and you can dry.
- I'll warm up the soup in the microwave.
- You’ll have to clean your sink every time after you use it.
- I can refill the soybean paste jars.
- You can use any type of vegetable that you want.

2 Interrogative Sentence

- Is supper ready yet?
- Is it too hot for you?
- Do you cook at home?
- Don't you have air-conditioning in your kitchen?
- Do you know what 'tsp' stands for? Show in your hand how much 1 tsp is.
- Will you put the silverware in the drawer?
- Tom, will you please load the dishwasher?
- Have you ever made some desert?
- Have you finished the soup yet?
- Should I get the salads and soups ready?
- Should I get the pigs' feet on the grill?
- Can you cook well? What?
- Can I open a window and get some ventilation in here?
- Can I taste it?
- Can you give me a hand?
- Can you get the salad ready?
- Can you use any kind of cabbage for this recipe?
- When will dinner be ready?
- Where should I put the canned goods?
- Why is there no water coming out when you turn on the faucet?
- How many ml(millilitres) are there in ¾ cup?
- How many bottles of hongju should we order?
- How would you know how much salt to use in this recipe?
- What shape is a head of cabbage?
- What ingredients do we need?

- What other ingredients do we need?
- What do you think 'baste' means?
- What's wrong with the drain?
- What kind of jeon do you like?
- What do you put on a dubu jorim?
- What music plays in your kitchen?
- What is the one ingredient you must have in your kitchen?
- What is the hardest part of your job?
- What is the best part of your job?
- What is your favorite childhood meal?
- What's the temperature?
- What are we making?
- What if it spills onto the table?
- Who is the best cook that you know?
- Who would you want to have dinner with?

3 Imperative Sentence

- Be careful! Don't touch the blade.
- Add enough flour to make a soft dough.
- Add a pinch of salt in it, please.
- Bake for 15 minutes, shaking the pan a few times.
- Barbeque 6-8 minutes per side depending on the thickness of your steaks.
- Baste from time to time if necessary.
- Beat in the eggs, one at a time, then add the vanilla.
- Blend until smooth and add soup.

- Boil a lot of water in a pot.
- Braise the beef cubes on all sides until well browned.
- Bring me some lettuce/more soup.
- Bring me the sanitizer bucket.
- Broil lamb for 3 minutes per side.
- Brown the onions well, but do not blacken.
- Lightly brush with 2 tbsp of sesame oil and serve hot.
- Check the blade and the tray.
- Check it out.
- Chop a medium onion into slivers.
- In a small bowl, combine ice water, egg and vinegar.
- Cook it till boiling.
- Core, pare, and thinly slice the apples.
- Cover it while cooking.
- Cover the burn with a clean, dry pad.
- Cover the dough thoroughly.
- Cream butter and sugar, and beat in eggs one at a time.
- Crush the almonds.
- Cut away from your body.
- Cut in the butter, using a pastry blender, until crumbly.
- Cut it into slices.
- Cut it into 2-inch long, very fine julienne strips.
- Cut out the cores and remove the skin.
- Deep fat fry them at 350 degrees for approximately 2 minutes until golden brown.
- Dice the onion.
- Do it like this.

- Dot the tops with butter and place in a greased baking dish.
- Dredge with flour and shake off any excess.
- Dry the dishes.
- Fold in egg whites using a rubber spatula.
- Fry mint leaves until the colour turns dark.
- Get some shrimp from the freezer.
- Grate the cauliflower.
- Grease a large flat baking sheet with olive oil.
- Grind the pepper as you need it.
- Grill 5 to 6 minutes - turning as needed.
- Julienne each vegetable into a uniform shape.
- Keep it clean.
- Knead with hands to blend thoroughly.
- Look at it.
- Marinate for 15 minutes.
- Mash the potatoes.
- Mince the garlic.
- Mix up the sugar, butter and salt in a mixing bowl while I heat up the milk.
- Mop the floor toward the drain.
- Open the sanitizer/the box.
- Quickly pan broil the steaks for 1 minute.
- Pan fry ground beef until light brown in skillet.
- Pare the brown skin from the meat with a very sharp knife.
- Peel the apple/the radish and cut them into small cubes.
- Poach salmon about 2 minutes per side.
- Pour floor cleanser and water into the bucket.

- Pour some water in the pan.
- Preheat the oven to 375 degrees 20 minutes before baking.
- Put the dirty dishes in the sink.
- Put the plates and saucers in the cupboard.
- Put the mushroom on the cutting(chopping) board.
- Put the cups and glasses in the other cupboard.
- Put some bread in the toaster.
- Put the knife in the dish rack.
- Put a mat under the cutting board.
- Put it back in the bucket.
- Put your hand in cold water.
- Pick up the knife.
- Place the veal on top of the noodles and add the red sauce.
- Put antiseptic on your wound.
- Remove the seeds and cube the flesh.
- Rinse the dishes before you put them in the dish washer.
- Roast it for 30-40 minutes.
- Saute the onion, garlic, and tomatoes.
- Say "hot stuff" next time.
- Lightly score the surface of the steaks with a knife.
- Scrape up any little bits adhering to the pan.
- Scald the milk, then let it come to room temperature.
- Serve the hot dish.
- Set the table.
- Show the manager the cut.
- Show him/her your wound.
- Shred the cabbage.

- Sift the baking powder on top of it.
- Slice the mushrooms.
- Slice the onion in circular shape.
- Shred the mushrooms/the cabbages.
- Simmer on very low heat for 10 hours.
- Spread a layer of brown sugar over the dough.
- Sprinkle the white sugar over top of the brown sugar.
- Stir constantly and do not boil.
- Stir fry pork until color changes.
- Strain the liquid through a cheesecloth several times.
- Just take off the ends.
- Take the dirty knife to the dish washers.
- Take the sauce to the cook.
- Take two table spoon crushed garlic.
- Throw the peels in the dustbin.
- Trim fat from steak and cut into 4 equal portions.
- Turn the fish/the meat.
- Turn the oven up to 450 degrees.
- Unplug the slicer.
- Use one squirt of dish detergent when you wash the dishes.
- Use the squeegee to push the water to the drain.
- Walk with the blade down and give it to the manager.
- Whip egg yolks in a mixing bowl until light and fluffy.
- Wrap it in a clean bandage.
- Please put the rice onto the stove.
- Pleas chop the onions.
- Please clean the shelf.

- Please close the refrigerator.
- Please put the silverware on the table.
- Please put a new roll of paper towels in the dispenser.
- Please get a bucket of soapy water for me.
- Please turn the meatball upside down.
- Don’t overcook!
- Don't hold the refrigerator door open.
- Don't put those bones in the garbage disposal.
- Don't chop the mushroom.
- Don't pick up the broken glass with your hands!
- Don't touch the handle on that hot pan!
- Do not microwave the egg!
- Let’s make cinnamon rolls.
- Lets’ stick(=put) them in the oven.
- Let me check the recipe.
- Let me show how to make chicken tacos.
- Let it rise a bit and bake the cinnamon rolls for 30 to 40 minutes.

REFERENCE

참고문헌

Retrieved Jan. 5, 2019 from https://www.youtube.com/watch?v=mwjv4_ZYrw0

Retrieved Jan. 3, 2019 from https://www.youtube.com/watch?v=08HF_yXDh2I

Retrieved Jan. 13, 2019 from https://www.youtube.com/watch?v=12AymqL58uA

Retrieved Jan. 13, 2019 from https://www.youtube.com/watch?v=W0-t04I04s4

Retrieved Jan. 4, 2019 from https://www.youtube.com/watch?v=6pdM6CIVFoo

Retrieved Jan. 3, 2019 from https://www.youtube.com/watch?v=80wEttfQAmY

Retrieved Jan. 3, 2019 from https://www.youtube.com/watch?v=6pdM6CIVFoo

Retrieved Jan. 5, 2019 from https://www.youtube.com/watch?v=DBSVGBwSiCU

Retrieved Jan. 13, 2019 from https://www.collinsdictionary.com/dictionary/

Retrieved Jan. 13, 2019 from https://www.youtube.com/watch?v=Wxac75IQ5y8

Retrieved Jan. 13, 2019 from https://www.youtube.com/watch?v=3bH4bOFVecc

편저자 약력

강경재

- 전북대학교 졸업(학사)
- 호원대학교 졸업(학사)
- 경기대학교 대학원 관광경영학과 졸업(경영학 석사)
- 경기대학교 대학원 관광경영학과 졸업(경영학 박사)

現 혜전대학교 호텔조리외식계열 교수
前 군산 미공군기지 제8헌병대대 언어전문관
경기대학교, 호원대학교, 남서울대학교, 혜전대학교, 혜천대학교, 군장공업대학교, 원광보건대학교 강사
혜전대학교 호텔조리계열 학부장
혜전대학교 호텔조리외식계열 계열장
혜전대학교 호텔조리외식계열 음료경영전공 전공장
혜전대학교 호텔조리외식계열 일식전공 전공장
혜전대학교 호텔조리외식계열 조리유학전공 전공장
혜전대학교 호텔조리외식계열 글로벌조리전공 전공장
혜전대학교 호텔조리외식계열 교수
혜전대학교 호텔조리과 교수

- 저서 : 신관광영어강독, 학문사(1998)
Hotel & Food Service Cuisine English, 백산출판사(1999)
Guide to the Student Chef, 대왕사(2001)
Guide to Culinary English, 대왕사(2003)
Guide to Food Styling English, 대왕사(2005)
Guide to Recipe for the Student Chef, 대왕사(2006)
Guide to Culinary and Foodservice English, LBH(2007)
Guide to Kitchen English, 백산출판사(2008)
Guide to Recipes of Oriental Cuisines, 대왕사(2009)
Guide to the Culinary Industry, 백산출판사(2010)
Guide to Culinary Readings(Ⅰ), 백산출판사(2012)
Guide to Culinary Readings(Ⅱ), 백산출판사(2012)
Guide to Culinary Readings(Ⅲ), 백산출판사(2013)
Guide to Practical English for Japanese Cuisine, 가담플러스(2014)
Guide to Practical English for Korean Cuisine, 백산출판사(2016)
Guide to Understanding the Culinary Industry, 백산출판사(2018)

- 논문 : 호텔 레스토랑의 데이터베이스 마케팅에 관한 연구 외 다수

저자와의
합의하에
인지첩부
생략

Guide to Practical English for Culinary Arts

2019년 2월 20일 초판 1쇄 인쇄
2019년 2월 25일 초판 1쇄 발행

편저자 강경재
펴낸이 진욱상
펴낸곳 백산출판사
교 정 편집부
본문디자인 구효숙
표지디자인 오정은

등 록 2017년 5월 29일 제406-2017-000058호
주 소 경기도 파주시 회동길 370(백산빌딩 3층)
전 화 02-914-1621(代)
팩 스 031-955-9911
이메일 edit@ibaeksan.kr
홈페이지 www.ibaeksan.kr

ISBN 979-11-89740-40-5 93740
값 13,000원